LUXURY HOUSES

COUNTRY

LUXURY HOUSES

COUNTRY

edited by Cristina Paredes Benítez

teNeues

Editor and texts: Cristina Paredes Benítez

Art Director: Mireia Casanovas Soley

Layout: Nil Solà Serra

Translations: Ana G. Cañizares (English)
Marion Westerhoff (French)
Martin Fischer (German)
Maurizio Siliato (Italian)

Produced by Loft Publications
www.loftpublications.com

Published by teNeues Publishing Group

teNeues Publishing Company
16 West 22nd Street, New York, NY 10010, USA
Tel.: 001-212-627-9090, Fax: 001-212-627-9511

teNeues Book Division
Kaistraße 18, 40221 Düsseldorf, Germany
Tel.: 0049-(0)211-994597-0, Fax: 0049-(0)211-994597-40

teNeues Publishing UK Ltd.
P.O. Box 402, West Byfleet, KT14 7ZF, Great Britain
Tel.: 0044-1932-403509, Fax: 0044-1932-403514

teNeues France S.A.R.L.
4, rue de Valence, 75005 Paris, France
Tel.: 0033-1-55 76 62 05, Fax: 0033-1-55 76 64 19

teNeues Iberica S.L.
Pso. Juan de la Encina 2–48, Urb. Club de Campo
28700 S.S.R.R., Madrid, Spain
Tel./Fax: 0034-91-65 95 876

www.teneues.com

ISBN-10: 3-8327-9061-6
ISBN-13: 978-3-8327-9061-5

© 2005 teNeues Verlag GmbH + Co. KG, Kempen

Printed in Spain

Bibliographic information published by
Die Deutsche Bibliothek. Die Deutsche Bibliothek lists
this publication in the Deutsche Nationalbibliografie;
detailed bibliographic data is available in the Internet
at http://dnb.ddb.de.

Contents

Introduction

The concept of luxury is both complex and diverse, and always subjective, given that what some may consider luxurious and exclusive may not be deemed so by others. At times, it may be a way of exhibiting great financial success or social status, and in other instances it is used to define the exclusive and authentic. There is no doubt, however, that luxury signifies all that is considered magnificent, unique, elegant, and of great distinction and quality, with as much regard to aesthetics as to the wealth of the used materials. Throughout history, the concept of luxury as a symbol of excellence has been expressed in architecture and art, as well as furniture and decorative objects.

This book presents splendid residences, villas and houses decorated with rich materials that are distinguished by opulence, elegance and in some cases, exoticism. The varied selection features predominantly rustic and classical styles, which are not at all contradictory to the concept of luxury. This provides an insight into the lifestyle and atmosphere experienced of luxurious country or beachfront living.

Life outside the city is at a slower pace, as rural or waterfront locations transmit a tranquility and peace not easily come by in large cities. These qualities are reflected in the interiors of the presented houses, creating exceptionally intimate and comfortable spaces that make the most out of time spent within the home or in company of family and friends in the garden and pool.

While elegance and sophistication are mainly reflected in the rich high-quality materials, luxury does not necessarily imply an exaggerated or formal decoration. The presented homes reflect the private lives of their owners. Country houses from around the world distinguished by their architecture and their refined and luxurious interiors, whose charm and selective décor prove to be as stunning as their respective exteriors, where mesmerizing gardens with spectacular views compel the onlooker to contemplate the landscape.

Einleitung

Luxus ist ein sehr vielschichtiger Begriff, der allerdings keinen absoluten Zustand bezeichnet, denn was für manche einen Luxus darstellt, kann für andere ganz alltäglich sein. Luxus wird oft mit der Vorstellung verbunden, dass jemand ein herausragendes Niveau erreicht, großen Reichtum erworben oder besonderes gesellschaftliches Ansehen erlangt hat. Aber das Wort steht auch für Exklusivität und Authentizität. Immerhin scheint Übereinstimmung dahingehend zu bestehen, dass als Luxus gilt, was hervorragend, einzigartig, elegant, distinguiert und von großer Qualität ist, und zwar nicht nur ästhetisch, sondern auch hinsichtlich der Auswahl der Materialen. Zu allen Zeiten war Luxus ein Ausdruck für eine herausgehobene Stellung. Er zeigt sich stets in der Architektur und der Kunst sowie in der Gestaltung von Möbeln und dekorativen Objekten.

Dieses Buch stellt Aufsehen erregende Häuser, Villen und Chalets vor, die mit ausgesuchten Materialien ausgestattet sind und sich durch Pracht, Eleganz und nicht selten durch Exotik auszeichnen. Trotz der Vielfalt der Stile überwiegen ländliche und klassische Interieurs, die mit der Vorstellung von Luxus keinesfalls unvereinbar sind. So erhält man vielfältige Einblicke in einen luxuriösen Lebensstil auf dem Land oder am Meer.

Fern der Stadt lebt es sich ruhiger. Die friedliche Stille der ländlichen Umgebung oder an der Küste wird man in einer Großstadt vergebens suchen. Das spiegelt sich auch in den Häusern wider: Einladende, gemütliche Räume lassen an verträumte Stunden am Kamin denken, und draußen bieten Garten und Schwimmbad Entspannung und Erfrischung, sei es im Kreise der Familie oder mit guten Freunden.

Eleganz und Exklusivität zeigen sich vor allem in den ausgesuchten Materialien hervorragender Qualität. Luxus muss nicht mit übertriebener Dekoration einhergehen. Die hier gezeigten Häuser spiegeln eine bestimmte Vorstellung von privaten Leben. In der ganzen Welt zeichnen sich Landhäuser durch ihre Architektur, ihren Luxus und die die geschmackvolle Gestaltung der Räume aus. Diese faszinieren durch ihren ganz eigenen Charme und die gepflegte Dekoration, während draußen die Gärten den Blick des Betrachters fesseln und wundervolle Landschaften dazu einladen, der Fantasie freien Lauf zu lassen.

Introduction

Le luxe est un concept complet et très varié, sans être pour autant une notion absolue, car ce qui pour certains est luxueux et exclusif ne l'est pas nécessairement pour d'autres. C'est parfois l'occasion d'afficher l'excellence du niveau de vie matériel, le prestige social ou encore la manière de définir ce qui est exclusif et authentique. Il semble toutefois qu'il y ait une définition universelle du luxe, qui englobe ce qui est magnifique, unique, élégant, hautement distingué et de qualité supérieure, tant par l'esthétique que par la richesse des matériaux. Au fil de l'histoire, le luxe dans le sens d'excellence, s'est exprimé au travers d'œuvres architecturales et artistiques, du mobilier et d'objets de décoration.

Ce livre présente des splendides résidences, villas et chalets agencés à l'aide de matériaux très riches, somptueux, resplendissant d'élégance et même d'exotisme. Les styles sont variés, avec une certaine prédominance des intérieurs rustiques et classiques, qui, à l'instar des exemples suivants, ne sont pas incompatibles avec la notion de luxe. En outre, il est aussi possible de déceler et de sentir le style de vie existant dans des lieux où le luxe côtoie la vie à la campagne ou à la plage.

Vivre hors de la ville, c'est changer de rythme de vie. Le calme et la paix qui se dégagent de l'environnement rural ou de la côte se trouvent difficilement dans les grandes cités et ceci se reflète dans l'agencement intérieur des maisons. Pièces extrêmement accueillantes et confortables propices à la découverte de ces instants particuliers à côté du foyer, de ces moments rafraîchissants et relaxants passés à la piscine ou au jardin en famille, avec des amis.

Elégance et subtilité se reflètent dans les matériaux haut de gamme et précieux. Le luxe ne correspond pas ici à une décoration formelle excessive : les maisons suivantes affichent une certaine idée de la vie dans l'environnement privé d'une résidence. Les maisons de campagne du monde entier se distinguent par leur architecture, le luxe et le bon goût de la décoration intérieure. Les intérieurs fascinent par leur charme et leur décoration particulièrement soignée. A l'extérieur, les jardins captivent le spectateur et les merveilleux paysages laissent vagabonder l'esprit au gré de l'imagination.

Introducción

El concepto de lujo es complejo y muy variado, aunque lo curioso es que no es una idea absoluta, pues lo que para algunos es lujoso y exclusivo puede no serlo para otros. En ocasiones, es una manera de mostrar a los demás que se ha alcanzado un alto nivel de excelencia, ya sea económico o de prestigio social, y en otras se emplea para definir lo que es exclusivo y auténtico. Donde sí parece haber consenso es en que lujo es todo aquello que se considera magnífico, único, elegante, de gran distinción y calidad, tanto por su estética como por la riqueza de los materiales que lo componen. A lo largo de la historia, la idea de lujo como excelencia se ha expresado mediante obras arquitectónicas y artísticas, mobiliario y objetos decorativos.

Este libro presenta espléndidas residencias, villas y chalés decorados con materiales de gran riqueza que desprenden suntuosidad, elegancia e incluso exotismo. Los estilos son variados, aunque predominan los interiores rústicos y clásicos, que, como puede comprobarse, no son incompatibles con el concepto de lujo. Además, en ellos es posible adivinar y sentir cómo es el estilo de vida en lugares donde el lujo convive con la vida en el campo o en la playa.

Vivir fuera de la ciudad significa disfrutar de otro ritmo de vida. La tranquilidad y la paz que transmiten el entorno rural o de costa resultan difíciles de encontrar en las grandes urbes, y esto se refleja en el interior de las casas. Estancias extremadamente acogedoras y cómodas descubren el gusto por esos instantes especiales junto al hogar o por esos refrescantes y relajantes momentos en la piscina y en el jardín en familia o con amigos.

La elegancia y sofisticación se reflejan en los materiales de excelente calidad y riqueza. El lujo no implica aquí una exagerada decoración formal; las casas que aparecen a continuación plasman una actitud vital en el entorno privado de una residencia. Casas de campo de todo el mundo se distinguen por su arquitectura y por el lujo y la adecuación de su decoración interior. Los interiores fascinan por su encanto y por su cuidadosa decoración; en el exterior, los jardines cautivan al espectador y los maravillosos paisajes consiguen hacer volar la imaginación.

Introduzione

Il concetto di lusso è complesso e molto vario, sebbene la cosa strana è che non si tratta di un'idea assoluta, visto che ciò è lussuoso ed esclusivo per alcuni può non esserlo per altri. In alcune occasioni, è una maniera per mostrare agli altri di aver raggiunto un elevato livello economico o di prestigio sociale, mentre altre volte si utilizza per definire ciò che è esclusivo ed autentico. A parte alcune divergenze di opinione, si è concordi nel definire lussuoso tutto ciò che si considera unico, elegante, di grande distinzione e qualità, sia da un punto di vista estetico che della ricchezza dei materiali che lo compongono. Negli anni, l'idea di lusso come eccellenza si è espressa mediante opere architettoniche ed artistiche, mobili e raffinati oggetti decorativi.

Questo volume presenta una serie di splendide dimore, ville e chalet arredati con materiali di qualità che sprigionano sontuosità, eleganza e persino esotismo. Gli stili sono svariati, sebbene predominano quelli rustici e classici che come sarà possibile constatare, non sono incompatibili con il concetto di lusso. Inoltre, percorrendo le varie residenze, è possibile indovinare e percepire come il lusso conviva con uno stile di vita rurale o tipico delle zone di mare.

Vivere fuori città significa, tra l'altro, godere di un altro stile e ritmo di vita. La tranquillità e la pace trasmessi dall'ambiente rurale o costiero sono difficili da trovare nelle grandi metropoli, e ciò si rispecchia negli interni delle case. Stanze estremamente accoglienti e comode fanno riscoprire il piacere di momenti speciali trascorsi in compagnia di amici o familiari accanto al focolare, alla piscina o in giardino.

L'eleganza e la raffinatezza vengono rispecchiate dai materiali estremamente ricchi e di qualità. Il lusso non implica in questi casi un'esagerata decorazione formale; le case che compaiono di seguito plasmano senza troppi sfarzi un ambiente elegante e allo stesso tempo intimo e familiare. Case situate in varie parti del mondo che si fanno notare per le loro soluzioni architettoniche e per l'arredamento degli interni, minuziosamente curato e adeguato alle circostanze. Gli interni affascinano per la loro accurata decorazione; all'esterno, i giardini e il meraviglioso panorama colpiscono i visitatori facendo volare l'immaginazione.

Classic Style in Madrid

☐ This residence in the outskirts of Madrid has a majestic flair. From the porch columns to the mouldings of the vaulted ceiling, all areas express elegance and extravagance. Beautiful floral motifs adorn the curtains and the upholstery of the sofas and armchairs, while the colors and furnishings differentiate the individual areas while maintaining a unified style. The dining room is decorated in elegant red tones while the living room is bathed in soft yellow and pink shades. The bathrooms are distinguished by their wallpaper, which is also used in other areas such as the office and dressing room, creating a sophisticated and exclusive atmospheres.

☐ In diesem Haus in der Nähe von Madrid spürt man ein herrschaftliches Flair. Die Säulen der Vorhalle, die Gesimse und die gewölbte Decke – alles vermittelt Pracht und Eleganz. Schöne Blumenmotive schmücken Vorhänge, Sofas und Sessel. Möbel und Farben werden so kombiniert, dass sich die einzelnen Räume voneinander unterscheiden, und zugleich ein einheitlicher Stil gewahrt bleibt. Das Speisezimmer ist in elegantem Rot gehalten, die Salons in zarten Gelb- und Rosatönen. Sowohl die Badezimmer als auch einige andere Bereiche, wie das Büro oder das Ankleidezimmer, sind tapeziert und gewinnen so einen exklusiven Charakter.

☐ Cette résidence de la banlieue de Madrid respire la majesté. Depuis les colonnes de l'atrium jusqu'aux moulures en passant par le toit voûté, les espaces de vie diffusent élégance et somptuosité. De merveilleux tissus décorés de motifs à fleurs parent les rideaux et les tapisseries des divans et fauteuils. Le mobilier et les couleurs se mêlent pour différencier les pièces à vivre, tout en gardant une unité de style. La salle à manger est décorée d'élégants tons rouges et les salons de doux jaunes et roses. Les salles de bains se distinguent grâce au papier peint des murs récurent dans le bureau et le dressing, créant une atmosphère exclusive et seigneuriale.

☐ En esta residencia de las afueras de Madrid se respira majestuosidad. Desde las columnas del porche hasta las molduras y el techo abovedado, las estancias transmiten elegancia y suntuosidad. Preciosas telas visten con motivos florales las cortinas y tapicerías de los sofás y butacas. El mobiliario y los colores se combinan para diferenciar las estancias, aunque mantienen un estilo unitario. El comedor está decorado con elegantes tonos rojos y los salones, con suaves amarillos y rosados. Los baños se distinguen por el papel pintado de las paredes, presentes también en otras estancias como el office y el vestidor, que crean atmósferas exclusivas y señoriales.

☐ In questa dimora situata fuori Madrid si respira una certa maestosità. A partire dalle colonne del porticato fino alle modanature e al soffitto a volta, i vari ambienti trasmettono eleganza e sontuosità. Delle tele pregiate vestono con motivi floreali le tende e la tappezzeria dei divani e delle poltrone. I mobili e i colori si abbinano tra loro per distinguere le varie stanze, pur mantenendo uno stile unitario. La sala da pranzo è decorata con eleganti tonalità rosse e i salotti, in tenui gialli e rosati. I bagni si distinguono per la carta da parati, presente anche in altri vani come l'ufficio e lo spogliatoio, che creano atmosfere esclusive e signorili.

Location: **Madrid, Spain**
Interior design: **Mónica Apponyi**
Photographer: **© Andreas von Einsiedel**

Feature space: **Main living room**

The main living room, decorated in shades of yellow, occupies a large living area with an arched ceiling. Thanks to their color, the upholstery and curtains generate a lively and intimate air. The light that enters through the small windows complements this tranquil and warm atmosphere.

Der große Salon mit seiner Rundbogendecke ist in gelblichen Tönen gehalten. Die Polsterbezüge und die Vorhänge mit ihren Farben lassen ihn so zu einem lebensfrohen, einladenden Ort werden. Das durch die kleinen Fenster dringende Licht trägt zu dieser ruhigen, warmen Atmosphäre bei.

Le salon principal, une grande pièce à vivre dotée d'un plafond en forme d'arc de plein cintre, décline les tons jaunes. La tapisserie et les rideaux créent, grâce à la couleur, un lieu accueillant et plein de vie. La lumière qui entre à travers les petites fenêtres parachève l'atmosphère chaleureuse et calme.

El salón principal, una gran estancia con el techo en forma de arco de medio punto, está decorado con tonos amarillos. La tapicería y las cortinas crean, gracias al color, un lugar acogedor y lleno de vida. La luz que entra a través de las pequeñas ventanas completa la tranquila y cálida atmósfera.

Il salone principale, una grande stanza con il soffitto a forma di arco a tutto sesto, è decorato in tonalità gialle. La tappezzeria e le tende creano, grazie ai colori, un posto accogliente e pieno di vita. La luce che entra attraverso le piccole finestre completa l'atmosfera calda e tranquilla.

In the library, a small area adjacent to the main living room features a large bookcase filled with elaborately bound volumes, while sofas and armchairs create comfortable reading areas within the cozy and sophisticated room.

In der neben dem Salon gelegenen kleinen Bibliothek fallen die riesigen Regale ins Auge, in denen Bücher mit aufwändigem Einband stehen. Sofas und Sessel bilden Leseecken in einem vornehmen Ambiente.

Dans la bibliothèque, petite salle attenante au salon principal, se détachent d'immenses étagères, accueillant des ouvrages aux reliures luxueuses. Les sofas et fauteuils créent des coins de lecture confortables au sein d'une pièce seigneuriale et accueillante.

En la biblioteca, una pequeña sala junto al salón principal, destacan unas enormes estanterías que alojan volúmenes con encuadernaciones de lujo; los sofás y butacas configuran cómodos rincones de lectura dentro de una estancia señorial y acogedora.

Nella biblioteca, una piccola sala accanto al salone principale, colpiscono l'occhio due enormi scaffalature contenenti volumi dalle pregiate rilegature; i divani e le poltrone compongono comodi angoli di lettura all'interno di una stanza signorile ed accogliente.

Residence in Majorca

☐ Majorca is one of the islands of the Balearic archipelago, known for its wonderful landscapes and Mediterranean climate. This elegantly decorated residence represents a rural way of life in a peaceful setting. Rustic architectural elements include the stone facade, the wooden beams and the robust front door. The interior is decorated and furnished in the traditional style; tables, chests of drawers and sideboards adorn the luxurious rooms like the bedroom, which accommodates an elegant canopy bed. The simplicity of the objects and the fine taste of the owner achieve a well-balanced design.

☐ Die Baleareninsel Mallorca ist vor allem für ihr mediterranes Klima und ihre fantastischen Landschaften bekannt. Dieses elegant dekorierte Haus steht für einen ländlichen Lebensstil in friedlicher Umgebung. Viele rustikale Bauelemente fallen ins Auge: die steinerne Fassade, die hölzernen Balken und das massive Eingangstor. Die Räume und ihre Ausstattung sind im traditionellen Stil gehalten; kleine Tische, Kommoden und Anrichten schmücken die großzügigen Zimmer. Ein elegantes Himmelbett beherrscht das Schlafzimmer. Dem Innenarchitekten ist es gelungen, mit Hilfe vieler schlichter Stücke einen ausgewogenen Gesamteindruck zu schaffen.

☐ Majorque est une île de l'archipel des Baléares, connue, entre autres choses, pour ses paysages merveilleux et pour son climat méditerranéen. Cette habitation, décorée avec élégance, évoque un style de vie rurale dans un environnement paisible. Les éléments rustiques de l'architecture sont présents sur la façade en pierre, les poutres de bois et la solide porte d'entrée. Les pièces gardent un style traditionnel, que l'on retrouve aussi dans le mobilier : petites tables, commodes et buffets ornent les espaces luxueux. Un lit élégant à baldaquin orne la chambre à coucher. L'harmonie est le fruit de la simplicité des pièces et du bon goût du décorateur.

☐ Mallorca es una isla del archipiélago balear conocida, entre otras cosas, por sus fantásticos paisajes y por su clima mediterráneo. Esta vivienda, decorada con elegancia, evoca un estilo de vida rural en un entorno apacible. Los elementos rústicos de la arquitectura son visibles en la fachada de piedra, en las vigas de madera y en la robusta puerta de entrada. Las estancias mantienen un estilo tradicional, también presente en el mobiliario; mesillas, cómodas y aparadores decoran lujosos espacios, y se ha ubicado una elegante cama con dosel en el dormitorio. El equilibrio se ha conseguido gracias a la sencillez de las piezas y al buen gusto del decorador.

☐ L'isola di Maiorca, la principale dell'arcipelago delle Baleari, è nota tra l'altro per i suoi fantastici paesaggi e per il clima mediterraneo. Questa abitazione, arredata con eleganza, evoca uno stile di vita rurale in un ambiente tranquillo. Gli elementi rustici dell'architettura sono visibili nella facciata in pietra, nelle travi in legno e nella robusta porta dell'entrata. Le stanze presentano uno stile tradizionale, comune anche alla mobilia; tavolini, cassettiere e credenze arredano spazi lussuosi; nella camera da letto è stato sistemato un letto con baldacchino. L'equilibrio si è ottenuto grazie alla semplicità dei pezzi e al buon gusto dell'arredatore.

Location: **Majorca, Spain**
Architect: **Holger Stewen**
Photographer: **© Andreas von Einsiedel**

Feature space: **Patio**

The patio allows the owner to enjoy the fresh air in privacy. Despite its fairly small size, the abundant foliage creates the perfect setting for soaking in the characteristic atmosphere of the island.

Der Patio erlaubt dem Besitzer entspannte Aufenthalte unter freiem Himmel. Obwohl er nicht sehr groß ist, bietet der von üppiger Vegetation erfüllte Innenhof einen diskreten Rückzugsort, an dem man den besonderen Geist der Insel ungestört auf sich einwirken lassen kann.

Le patio intérieur permet de bénéficier d'une certaine intimité et de moments délicieux à l'air libre. Malgré ses dimensions modestes, cet endroit rempli de végétation, paisible et discret, permet de s'imprégner de l'esprit et de l'ambiance particulière de l'île.

El patio interior permite disfrutar de intimidad y de agradables ratos al aire libre. A pesar de que sus dimensiones no son demasiado grandes, está repleto de vegetación y es un lugar apacible y discreto donde empaparse del espíritu y del ambiente especial de la isla.

Il cortile interno consente di trascorrere piacevoli momenti all'aria aperta e in assoluta privacy. Nonostante le sue ridotte dimensioni, la ricca vegetazione ne fa un luogo tranquillo e discreto dove impregnarsi dello spirito e del singolare ambiente che si respira nell'isola.

The patio is connected to a roofed porch, containing the dining area and an old sofa, that provides a pleasant and intimate setting in which to enjoy nature and contemplate the gardens during dinner parties or morning breakfast.

An den Patio grenzt ein halboffener, überdachter Raum. Hier wurde ein Essplatz eingerichtet und ein altes Sofa aufgestellt und so ein geschützter Platz geschaffen, an dem man während eines Frühstücks oder eines Abendessens im Sommer die schönen Gärten genießen kann, ohne den Unbilden der Witterung ausgesetzt zu sein.

Le patio est uni à un porche couvert, accueillant une salle à manger extérieure et un vieux divan, est un espace qui permet de profiter de l'extérieur tout en étant en retrait, et de se régaler, à l'abri des intempéries, en contemplant les magnifiques jardins et en dégustant de délicieux dîners estivaux ou des petits déjeuners à l'air libre.

El patio está conectado a un porche cubierto, donde se ha ubicado un comedor exterior y un antiguo sofá; es un espacio que permite disfrutar del exterior y a la vez de cierto recogimiento, y deleitarse, sin estar completamente a la intemperie, contemplando los hermosos jardines mientras se disfruta de cenas veraniegas o desayunos al aire libre.

Il patio è collegato a un porticato copertó, che consente di pranzare e cenare all'aperto, è un'oasi di tranquillità dove poter godersi la vista dei giardini esterni e trascorrere, al riparo dalle intemperie, piacevoli momenti in compagnia sia di giorno che di sera.

The kitchen maintains the home's traditional atmosphere: typical objects from the area such as ceramic and clay plates, vases, jugs and cups are displayed on wooden shelves, while an old-fashioned oven and a wrought iron lamp fixture complement the general picture.

In der Küche kann man noch die traditionelle Atmosphäre verspüren: Teller, Krüge und Tassen aus typisch mallorquinischer Keramik stehen auf den Holzregalen. Ein alter Backofen und eine schmiedeeiserne Lampe passen sich gut in das Gesamtbild ein.

La cuisine est un lieu qui conserve une atmosphère traditionnelle: assiettes, cruches jarres et tasses en céramiques et faïences typiques de la zone sont placées sur des étagères en bois. Un ancien fourneau et une lampe de forge parachèvent l'esthétique de la pièce.

La cocina es un lugar que conserva una atmósfera tradicional: platos, jarrones, jarras y tazas de cerámica y loza típica de la zona están colocados sobre unos estantes de madera, y un horno antiguo y una lámpara de forja completan la estética de la estancia.

La cucina è l'ambiente dove si respira di più l'atmosfera tradizionale. Piatti, vasi, brocche e tazze in ceramica e maiolica tipica della zona sono disposti su degli scaffali in legno; completano il tocco rustico della stanza un forno antico e una lampada in ferro battuto.

Southern Charm

☐ This magnificent residence situated in Atlanta evokes the southern charm of 19th century America. The splendor of the house can be felt every one of its rooms, each detail is painstakingly conceived to create a warm, comfortable atmosphere. Comfortable sofas upholstered in quality materials, bureaux, wooden furnishings and decorative objects like the ceramics of different styles are tastefully combined. The kitchen is the place in which to enjoy the warmth of the home and spend time with family. Large glass doors, which allow the daylight to bathe a small rustic dining area, lead outside.

☐ Dieses wunderbare Anwesen liegt in Atlanta und beschwört die Südstaaten des 19. Jhs. wieder herauf. Der Glanz des Hauses ist in allen Räumen zu verspüren, alles ist bis ins kleinste Detail durchdacht, um eine äußerst angenehme und behagliche Atmosphäre zu schaffen. Hochwertig gepolsterte Sofas, Kommoden, Vollholzmöbel und dekorative Gegenstände, wie die Keramik verschiedener Stile, sind geschmackvoll miteinander kombiniert. In der Küche genießt man die Wärme des Herdfeuers und trifft sich mit der Familie. Das kleine Esszimmer mit den rustikalen Möbeln erhält sein helles Licht durch Glastüren, die ins Freie führten.

☐ Cette superbe résidence, située à Atlanta, évoque l'Amérique méridionale du XIXeme siècle. La splendeur de la maison est présente dans toutes les pièces, objets d'un soin méticuleux, elles sont chaleureuses et extrêmement confortables. Divans tapissés de tissus de qualité, commodes, mobilier de bois et objets de décoration se marient avec goût, à l'instar de la céramique de styles différents. La cuisine est un espace où l'on profite de la chaleur du logis et où la famille se réunit. Des verrières conduisant a l'extérieur qui inondent de lumière une petite salle à manger formée d'éléments de meubles rustiques.

☐ Esta magnífica residencia situada en Atlanta evoca la América sureña del siglo XIX. El esplendor de la casa está presente en todas sus estancias, minuciosamente cuidadas para crear ambientes cálidos y extremadamente confortables. Sofás de tapicerías de calidad, cómodas, mobiliario de madera y objetos decorativos se combinan con gusto, como la cerámica, de diferentes estilos. La cocina es un espacio en el que disfrutar del calor del hogar y donde reunirse en familia. Se accede al exterior a través de unas cristaleras, que inundan de luz un pequeño comedor formado por piezas de mobiliario rústicas.

☐ Questa magnifica residenza situata ad Atlanta evoca immagini dell'America del sud del XIX secolo. Lo stile sontuoso è presente in tutte le stanze della casa, curate nei minimi particolari per dar vita a degli ambienti accoglienti ed estremamente confortevoli. Sofà tappezzati con stoffe pregiate, comò e altri mobili in legno, oggetti decorativi sono combinati con gusto, al pari della ceramica, in stili diversi tra loro. La cucina costituisce uno spazio di ritrovo accogliente per tutta la famiglia. Si accede all'esterno attraverso le vetrate che inondano di luce una piccola sala da pranzo arredata con pezzi rustici.

Location: **Atlanta, Georgia, USA**
Architect: **Joan Brendle**
Photographer: © **Andreas von Einsiedel**

Feature space: Bedroom

The bedroom is one of the most thoughtfully designed areas of the residence. It includes a small reading area with armchairs and stairs that lead to the upper floor. The warmth of this bedroom is further enhanced by its elegant, high quality furnishings.

Das Schlafzimmer ist einer der Räume mit einer besonders gepflegten Einrichtung. Es besitzt einen Bereich mit Sesseln zum Lesen und einer Treppe, die ins Obergeschoss führt. Die wertvollen Möbel verleihen diesem eleganten Raum eine anheimelnde Atmosphäre.

La chambre à coucher est une des pièces où le décor est extrêmement soigné. Elle possède un petit salon avec des fauteuils en guise de zones de lecture et des escaliers qui conduisent à l'étage supérieur. Elégante et parée d'un mobilier de grande qualité cette chambre transmet la chaleur du foyer.

El dormitorio es una de las estancias con una decoración más cuidada. Incluye un pequeño salón con butacas como zona de lectura y unas escaleras que conducen al piso superior. Elegante y con un mobiliario de gran calidad, esta habitación transmite calor de hogar.

La camera da letto è una delle stanze che è stata arredata con particolare attenzione. Questa include un piccolo angolo lettura con poltrone e delle scale che conducono al piano superiore. Elegante e con dei mobili di ottima qualità, questa stanza trasmette intimità e calore.

The dining area is situated between the staircase that leads to the upper floor and the living room. This unique layout lends a dynamic quality to the individual areas. This is also reflected in the shapes and colors of the decoration.

Das Speisezimmer liegt zwischen der Treppe, die in den ersten Stock führt, und dem Wohnzimmer. Durch diese eigenwillige Anordnung stehen die Innenräume immer in einer dynamischen Verbindung. Verstärkt wird dieser Eindruck durch die Innenausstattung, deren Formen und Farben sich in perfekten Harmonie zusammenfügen.

La salle à manger est située entre l'escalier qui conduit au premier étage et au salon. Cette distribution particulière est dynamique et crée une communication permanente entre les intérieurs. La décoration en bénéficie également avec des couleurs et des formes qui cohabitent en parfaite harmonie.

El comedor está situado entre la escalera que conduce al primer piso y el salón. Esta particular distribución aporta dinamismo y hace que los interiores se relacionen en todo momento. La decoración también se beneficia de ello, ya que consigue cohesionar formas y colores.

La sala da pranzo si trova tra la rampa di scale che porta al primo piano e il salone. Questa peculiare distribuzione apporta dinamismo e fa sì che gli interni si relazionino in ogni momento. Di ciò si avvantaggia anche l'arredamento, in grado di fondere forme e colori.

Farm in Africa

☐ This magnificent colonial-style residence is located in the outskirts of Cape Town, but only a small number of decorative objects give away its location. It's simple decoration indicates exquisite taste through the use of quality materials, and a balance of forms. Elegant and somewhat sober furnishings were chosen, creating a distinguished air contemporary atmosphere. The unique floors link the one of the living areas to the bedrooms, while the delicate earth and green shades of the bathroom tiles create a natural and warm space. A large exterior porch offers a magnificent view of the landscape.

☐ Dieses herrliche Anwesen im Kolonialstil befindet sich in der Nähe von Kapstadt, doch nur einige wenige dekorative Elemente weisen auf diesen Standort hin. Die schlicht gehaltene Einrichtung mit erstklassigen Materialien und einem gelungenen Gleichgewicht der Formen lässt auf einen vortrefflichen Geschmack schließen. Das Mobiliar der einzelnen Räume ist elegant, ja fast nüchtern, und schafft eine distinguierte zeitgemäße Atmosphäre. Der originale Bodenbelag verbindet die Wohnräume mit den Schlafzimmern. Die dezenten Fliesen im Bad mit ihren Erd- und Grüntönen vermitteln ein Gefühl natürlicher Wärme. Vom Portikus aus hat man einen weiten Blick.

☐ Cette magnifique résidence de style coloniale est située dans les faubourgs de la Ville du Cap. Toutefois, quelques objets décoratifs trahissent son emplacement. Très simplement décorée, avec beaucoup de goût, elle est dotée de matériaux de qualité et de formes parfaitement harmonieuses. Le mobilier choisi pour les espaces de vie est à la fois élégant et sobre, créant une ambiance distinguée et contemporaine. Le sol d'origine unifie les salons et les chambres à coucher. Les subtiles céramiques de la salle de bains déclinant les tons terre de sienne et vert, définissent un espace naturel et chaud. A l'extérieur, un grand porche encadre de merveilleuses vues.

☐ Esta magnífica residencia de estilo colonial se halla en las afueras de Ciudad del Cabo; sin embargo, tan sólo unos pocos objetos decorativos delatan su emplazamiento. Presenta una decoración sencilla que hace gala de un gusto exquisito, unos materiales de calidad y un acertado equilibrio en las formas. El mobiliario escogido para las estancias es elegante y algo sobrio, y crea un ambiente distinguido y contemporáneo. El original suelo une los salones con los dormitorios; las delicadas baldosas del baño en tonos tierra y verde configuran un espacio natural y cálido. En el exterior, un gran porche ofrece agradables vistas.

☐ Questa magnifica dimora dallo stile coloniale si trova alla periferia di Città del Capo; ciò nonostante, soltanto pochi oggetti decorativi rivelano la sua ubicazione. È stata arredata in maniera semplice ma con gusto e raffinatezza; presenta dei materiali di qualità e un giusto equilibrio nelle forme. La mobilia scelta per le stanze è elegante e alquanto sobria, e crea un ambiente distinto e contemporaneo. L'originale pavimento unisce i saloni con le camere da letto; le delicate piastrelle del bagno in toni terra e verde danno vita a uno spazio naturale e accogliente. All'esterno, un gran porticato offre piacevoli viste panoramiche.

Location: **Cape Town, South Africa**
Architects: **Steven Harris Architects & Lucien Rees-Roberts**
Photographer: © **Andreas von Einsiedel**

Feature space: **Living room**

The residence's exterior allows the residents to enjoy the natural setting. Underneath the porch, the wicker chairs create a cozy ambience, while the wooden deck with its colonial-style chairs form an open and natural space that blends into the surrounding landscape.

In den Außenanlagen kann man die Natur der Umgebung genießen. Die Rohrstühle unter dem Vordach schaffen eine gemütliche Atmosphäre und das hölzerne Podest mit den Stühlen im Kolonialstil bilden einen offenen, naturnahen Raum, der mit der Umgebung verschmilzt.

Les espaces extérieurs permettent de bénéficier de la nature environnante. Sous le porche, les fauteuils en osier créent une ambiance accueillante et le banc en lattes de bois à côté des sièges de style colonial forment un espace ouvert et naturel qui se fond dans l'environnement.

Los espacios exteriores permiten disfrutar de la naturaleza de los alrededores. Bajo el porche, los sillones de mimbre crean un ambiente acogedor y la tarima de láminas de madera junto con las sillas de estilo colonial forman un espacio abierto y natural que se fusiona con el entorno.

Gli spazi esterni consentono di godere della natura dei dintorni. Sotto il porticato, le poltrone di vimini creano un ambiente accogliente e la pedana in legno lamellare assieme alle sedie in stile coloniale formano uno spazio aperto e naturale che si fonde con l'ambiente circostante.

The floors and wooden roof unite the different areas of the large living room. Sofas in different styles are combined with chests of drawers, side tables and decorative objects. Several contemporary artworks adorn the walls of this modern and elegant room.

Die hölzerne Decke und der Bodenbelag vereinen die verschiedenen Bereiche des großen Salons, in dem Sofas unterschiedlicher Stile, Kommoden, Beistelltische und dekorative Objekte kombiniert sind. Die Wände dieses eleganten, modernen Raums zieren Werke zeitgenössischer Künstler.

Le plafond boisé et le carrelage unifient les divers univers du grand salon. Divans de styles divers se conjuguent aux commodes, tables d'appoint et objets de décoration. Diverses œuvres d'art contemporain parent les murs de cet espace moderne et élégant.

La cubierta de madera y el pavimento unifican los diversos ambientes del gran salón. Sofás de estilos diferentes se combinan con cómodas, mesas auxiliares y objetos decorativos. Varias obras de arte contemporáneo visten las paredes de este espacio moderno y elegante.

La copertura in legno e il pavimento unificano i diversi ambienti del grande salone. Sofà in stili diversi si abbinano a cassettiere, tavoli supplementari e oggetti decorativi. Varie opere d'arte contemporanea addobbano le pareti di questo spazio moderno ed elegante.

Swiss Precision

☐ This luxurious mountain chalet is warm and elegant. The fabrics and furnishings combine delicately to create a comfortable interior. The neutral tones of the upholstery and furniture pieces from different periods lend a distinguished air to the house that was conceived as a winter retreat. The large kitchen and main bathroom are examples of how simplicity can also be captivating. The main living room is one of the most comfortable areas of the home: a large sofa and leather armchair create a markedly warm atmosphere. The windows and tall ceilings emphasize the spaciousness of the living area, which is the ideal place for gatherings and celebrations.

☐ Dieses luxuriöse Chalet in den Bergen ist gemütlich und elegant zugleich. Hier wurden Stoffe und Möbelstücke geschmackvoll kombiniert, um ein einladendes Interieur zu schaffen. Die neutralen Töne der Bezugsstoffe und die Möbel verschiedener Stilepochen verleihen der als Winterquartier gedachten Wohnung einen distinguierten Charakter. Die große Küche und das Badezimmer bestechen durch ihre Einfachheit. Das Wohnzimmer ist einer der gemütlichsten Räume: ein großes Sofa und ein Ledersessel schaffen eine anheimelnde Atmosphäre. Die Fenster und die hohe Decke verstärken den Eindruck von Weite und machen den Raum zu einem idealen Rahmen für Zusammenkünfte und Feiern.

☐ Ce chalet de montagne luxueux est à la fois chaleureux et élégant. Les tissus et le mobilier se marient avec délicatesse et bon goût pour créer un intérieur confortable. Les tons neutres des tapisseries et les meubles de différentes époques confèrent un air distingué à la demeure, conçue pour y passer la saison hivernale. La grande cuisine et la salle de bains principale sont deux exemples qui montrent combien la simplicité peut fasciner le visiteur. Le salon principal est une des pièces les plus accueillantes : un grand divan et un fauteuil en cuir créent une ambiance très chaleureuse. Les baies vitrées et l'importante hauteur du toit agrandissent le salon qui devient un lieu idéal pour réunions et cérémonies.

☐ Este lujoso chalé de montaña es cálido y elegante. Las telas y el mobiliario se combinan con delicadeza y gusto para crear un interior confortable. Los tonos neutros de las tapicerías y los muebles de diferentes épocas dan un aire distinguido a la vivienda, pensada para disfrutar de la temporada de invierno. La gran cocina y el baño principal son dos ejemplos de cómo la sencillez puede cautivar al visitante. El salón principal es una de las estancias más acogedoras: un gran sofá y una butaca de piel crean una atmósfera muy cálida. Los ventanales y la gran altura del techo aportan amplitud al salón, que se convierte en el lugar ideal para reuniones y celebraciones.

☐ Questo lussuoso chalet di montagna è accogliente ed elegante. Le tele e la mobilia sono abbinate con gusto e delicatezza e creano degli interni davvero confortevoli. I toni neutri della tappezzeria e i mobili di epoche diverse danno un tocco di distinzione all'abitazione, pensata per godere della stagione invernale. La grande cucina e il bagno principale sono due esempi di come persino la semplicità può affascinare il visitatore. Il salone principale è una delle stanze più accoglienti: un grande divano e una poltrona in pelle creano un'atmosfera molto ospitale. I finestroni e la gran altezza del soffitto danno ampiezza al salone che diventa così un luogo ideale per riunioni e celebrazioni

Location: **Zumikon, Switzerland**
Interior design: **Sue Rohrer**
Photographer: © **Zapaimages**

Feature space: **Bedroom**

A dark color was chosen for the bedroom walls, rugs and furnishings. However, the elegant bedspread and comfortable pillows, along with a well-devised illumination, create a cozy and distinguished atmosphere.

Die Wände, der Teppich und die Möbel des Schlafzimmers sind dunkel gehalten. Trotzdem entsteht durch die elegante Tagesdecke und die bequemen Kissen mit Hilfe der ausgeklügelten Beleuchtung ein vornehm behaglicher Raum.

Les murs de la chambre à coucher sont foncés, à l'instar des meubles et tapis. Toutefois, l'élégant couvre-lit et les coussins confortables, associés à une répartition parfaite de l'éclairage, créent une pièce distinguée et accueillante.

Las paredes del dormitorio son de color oscuro, al igual que la alfombra y los muebles. Sin embargo, la elegante colcha y los confortables almohadones, junto con la acertada distribución de la iluminación, crean una estancia distinguida y acogedora.

Le pareti della stanza da letto sono di colore scuro, come il tappeto e i mobili. Ciò nonostante, l'elegante copriletto e i comodi guanciali, assieme ad un'accurata distribuzione della luce, creano una stanza singolare ed accogliente.

The combination of elements and textures is constantly present in this residence. The piping was left exposed in the bathroom and in the kitchen fragments of wine boxes were used to decorate the drawers, giving a unique and very personal touch.

Überall in diesem Haus findet man die Mischung von Elementen und Texturen. Im Badezimmer wurden die Leitungen auf Putz verlegt, und in der Küche wurden die Vorderseiten der Schubläden aus Weinkisten gefertigt – ein originelle, sehr persönliche Lösung.

Le mélange d'éléments et de textures est une constante de cette résidence. Dans la salle de bains, les tuyaux sont apparents et dans la cuisine des morceaux de caisses de vin servent de parement frontal aux tiroirs, ajoutant ainsi une touche originale, très personnelle.

La mezcla de elementos y texturas es una constante en esta residencia. En el baño, las tuberías quedan a la vista y en la cocina se han dispuesto fragmentos de cajas de vino como frontales de los cajones, lo que le da un toque original y muy personal.

La mescolanza di elementi e di texture è costante in questa residenza. Nel bagno, le tubature rimangono a vista e in cucina si sono collocati dei frammenti di scatole di vino come frontali dei cassetti, una soluzione che dà alla stanza un tocco originale e molto personale.

Retreat in the Country

☐ The renovation of this house in the Aquitaine region of France preserved its rustic interiors while adding a modern touch. This lavish residence is an example of the contemporary concept of luxury. The refreshing quality and vitality of the rooms create an evocative and luminous atmosphere. The main bedroom is situated on a modern mezzanine, while the wooden ceiling and beams as well as the structural elements and vaulted niches of one of the bedrooms were restored. The rather classical furnishings such as sofas and side tables are combined with contemporary items such as the table and chairs.

☐ Bei der Umgestaltung dieses Hauses in der französishen Aquitaine wurden die rustikalen Innenräume erhalten, wenn auch modernisiert. Das prachtvolle Haus zeigt, was man heute unter Luxus versteht. Durch die Frische und Lebendigkeit der Räume entsteht eine helle, zum Träumen anregende Atmosphäre. Das Schlafzimmer der Hausherrn wurde in einem modernen Zwischengeschoss untergebracht, die Holzdecken und Balken wurden ebenso wie die fest eingemauerten Möbel und die Wandnischen in einem der Schlafzimmer restauriert. Beim Mobiliar werden auf gelungene Weise heutige Stücke, wie der Tisch und die Stühle, mit eher klassischen Sofas und Beistelltischen auf Kapitellen kombiniert.

☐ La restauration de cette maison de la région française d'Aquitaine a conservé les intérieurs rustiques tout en apportant une vision plus moderne. Cette somptueuse résidence est un exemple de concept de luxe revisité. La fraîcheur et la vitalité des pièces créent une atmosphère évocatrice et lumineuse. La chambre de maîtres est installée dans une mansarde moderne. Les plafonds boisés et les poutres ont été restaurés, ainsi que les meubles d'art et les niches d'une des chambres à coucher. Le mobilier mêle avec art des meubles contemporains, comme la table et les fauteuils, à des divans de style plus classique et à des chapiteaux qui servent de pied de tables d'appoint.

☐ La remodelación de esta casa de la región francesa de Aquitania ha conservado los interiores rústicos pero aportando una visión más moderna. Esta suntuosa residencia es un ejemplo de lo que se obtiene al revisar el concepto de lujo. La frescura y vitalidad de las estancias crean una atmósfera evocadora y luminosa. El dormitorio principal se ha colocado en un moderno altillo y se han rehabilitado los techos de madera y las vigas, así como los muebles de obra y las hornacinas de uno de los dormitorios. El mobiliario combina con acierto muebles actuales, como la mesa y las sillas, con sofás de corte más clásico y capiteles que hacen de pies de mesas auxiliares.

☐ La ristrutturazione di questa casa della regione francese dell'Aquitania ha conservato gli interni rustici apportando però una visione più moderna. Questa sontuosa residenza simboleggia il risultato che si ottiene rivedendo il concetto di lusso. La freschezza e la vitalità delle stanze creano un'atmosfere evocativa e luminosa. La camera da letto principale è stata sistemata su un moderno soppalco, il soffitto e le travi in legno sono stati recuperati, così come i mobili in muratura e le nicchie di una delle camere da letto. La mobilia abbina in modo ben riuscito pezzi attuali, come la tavola e le sedie, con sofà dallo stile più classico e capitelli che fanno da supporto a tavoli supplementari.

Location: **Aquitaine, France**
Interior design: **Avril Delahunty**
Photographer: © **Andreas von Einsiedel**

Feature space: **Bedroom**

The mezzanine creates an additional space to observe the living room with a certain degree of intimacy. A unique bed with a leather-lined structure constitutes the room's main decorative object. The beams and wooden roof bestow great warmth to this open space.

Von der eingezogenen Empore aus kann man das Wohnzimmer überschauen, ohne dass man auf das Gefühl von Intimität verzichten müsste. Dekoratives Hauptelement ist ein originelles Bett, dessen Fuß- und Kopfteil mit Leder bezogen ist. Die Balken und die Holzdecke verleihen diesem offenen Raum Wärme.

La mansarde crée un espace supplémentaire donnant sur le salon, tout en conservant un certain degré d'intimité. Un lit original avec des pieds et une tête de lit doublés de cuir, est en lui-même un objet de décoration. Les poutres et le plafond boisé confèrent une ambiance chaleureuse à cet espace ouvert.

El altillo crea un espacio añadido desde el que se puede contemplar la sala, manteniendo cierto grado de intimidad. Una original cama con pies y cabecera forrados con piel constituye en sí misma un objeto decorativo. Las vigas y la cubierta de madera aportan calidez a este espacio abierto.

Il soppalco crea uno spazio aggiunto da cui è possibile osservare la sala, pur mantenendo un certo grado di intimità. L'originale letto con i piedi e la testata foderati in pelle costituisce di per sé un oggetto di decorazione. Le travi e il soffitto in legno conferiscono una nota di calore a questo spazio aperto.

The vaulted niches in the bedroom accentuate the rural atmosphere of the home and house numerous decorative objects from different places. The use of white contrasts with the warmth of the wooden beams and bed, creating a relaxed and tranquil atmosphere ideal for repose.

Die Nischen im Schlafzimmer unterstreichen den ländlichen Charakter des Hauses und bilden den Rahmen für zahlreiche dekorative Objekte aus aller Welt. Die weiße Farbe kontrastiert mit der Wärme der Balken und des Bettes, so dass eine entspannte ruhige Atmosphäre entsteht, die zum Schlafen einlädt.

Les niches de la chambre à coucher exaltent l'atmosphère rurale de la maison et mettent en valeur de nombreux objets de décoration d'origines diverses. Le blanc contraste avec la chaleur du bois des poutres et du lit, créant une ambiance détendue et calme, idéale pour se reposer.

Las hornacinas del dormitorio acentúan la atmósfera rural de la casa y muestran numerosos objetos decorativos de procedencia diversa. El color blanco contrasta con la calidez de la madera de las vigas y la cama, y crea un ambiente relajado y tranquilo, perfecto para el descanso.

Le nicchie della camera da letto accentuano l'atmosfera rurale della casa e mostrano numerosi soprammobili di diversa provenienza. Il bianco contrasta con i toni caldi delle travi e del lettó, e crea un ambiente rilassato e tranquillo, molto adatto al riposo.

Country Feel

This luxurious residence, situated on the outskirts of Zurich, features a delicate combination of styles and materials. Although it is not rustic in style, small details give away its countryside location. The elegant curtains and upholstery create a noble and distinguished ambience, as can be noted in the hallways and in areas like the reading area with armchairs next to the library. Various lamps were chosen for the illumination, while the silver walls prove an attractive contrast to the furnishings. Despite the variety of styles and colors, decorator manage to create a cohesive balance.

In diesem Haus in der Nähe von Zürich werden Stile und Materialien behutsam kombiniert. Obwohl es nicht im ländlichen Stil eingerichtet ist, verraten kleine Details der Dekoration seine Lage. Die eleganten Stoffe der Gardinen, Decken und Bezüge tragen dazu bei, ein vornehmes Ambiente zu schaffen, wie man etwa in den Übergangsbereichen oder bei den Sesseln in einer Ecke nahe der Bibliothek feststellen kann. Eine Vielzahl von Lampen sorgt für die Ausleuchtung; die silbernen Wände bilden einen kontrastreichen Hintergrund für die klassischen Möbel. Trotz der Vielfalt von Stilen und Farben ist es der Innenarchitektin gelungen, in den Räumen ein stimmiges geschmackvolles Gleichgewicht zu schaffen.

Cette demeure luxueuse, située aux alentours de Zurich, offre un mélange subtil de styles et de matériaux. Sans être de style rustique, certains petits détails dans la décoration trahissent son emplacement. Les élégants tissus de rideaux et tapisseries créent une ambiance seigneuriale et distinguée, comme on peut l'observer dans les zones de passage et dans les fauteuils d'un coin près de la bibliothèque. Des nombreuses lampes assurent l'éclairage, et les murs argentés contrastent avec de splendides meubles classiques. Malgré une grande variété de styles et de couleurs, les espaces restent harmonieux, grâce au talent particulier de la décoratrice.

Esta lujosa vivienda, situada en los alrededores de Zurich, muestra una delicada combinación de estilos y materiales. A pesar de no tener un estilo rústico, hay pequeños detalles en la decoración que delatan su emplazamiento. Los elegantes tejidos de cortinas y tapicerías crean un ambiente señorial y distinguido, como se puede observar en las zonas de paso y en las butacas de un rincón próximo a la biblioteca. Para la iluminación, se han colocado numerosas lámparas, y las paredes plateadas contrastan con espléndidos muebles de corte clásico. A pesar de la variedad de estilos y colores en las estancias, existe cohesión y equilibrio entre los espacios como resultado del particular gusto de la decoradora.

Questa lussuosa abitazione, situata nei dintorni di Zurigo, mostra una delicata combinazione di stili e materiali. Nonostante non presenti uno stile rustico, vi sono piccoli indizi dell'arredamento da cui è possibile capire la zona in cui si trova. Gli eleganti tessuti delle tende e in genere di tutta la tappezzeria creano un ambiente signorile e raffinato, come si può osservare nelle zone di passaggio e nelle poltrone di un angolo vicino alla biblioteca. In quanto all'illuminazione, sono state collocate numerose lampade, e le pareti argentate contrastano con splendidi mobili di taglio classico. Nonostante la varietà di stili e di colori presenti nelle stanze, esiste una certa coesione ed equilibrio tra gli spazi come risultato del peculiare gusto dell'arredatrice.

Location: **Zurich, Switzerland**
Interior design: **Sue Rohrer**
Photographer: © **Agi Simôes / Zapaimages**

Feature space: Reading corner

Halfway between the living room and the dining area, a table and various armchairs were placed next to a library with silver shelves containing elaborately bound volumes, thus creating a small, elegant corner ideal for reading or discussing literature.

Auf halbem Wege zwischen dem Wohn- und dem Esszimmer wurden ein Tisch und einige Sessel aufgestellt. Zusammen mit einem Bücherschrank, in dessen silbernen Regalen kunstvoll eingebundene Bücher stehen, ist so eine kleine ruhige Leseecke entstanden, in der man entspannt lesen oder mit Gleichgesinnten angeregt über Literatur plaudern kann.

A mi-chemin entre le salon et la zone de la salle à manger, l'espace est ponctué d'une table et de quelques fauteuils, à côté d'une bibliothèque aux étagères argentées qui contient des volumes parés de reliures luxueuses, créant ainsi un petit recoin élégant et tranquille, pour parler sur la littérature ou se plonger confortablement dans la lecture d'un livre.

A medio camino entre el salón y la zona del comedor, se han colocado una mesa y varias butacas, junto a una librería con estantes plateados que contienen volúmenes lujosamente encuadernados, y se ha creado así un pequeño rincón elegante y tranquilo, donde conversar sobre literatura o disfrutar cómodamente de la lectura.

A metà strada tra il salone e la zona della sala da pranzo, è stato collocato un tavolo e varie poltrone, accanto a una libreria con scaffali argentati contenenti volumi raffinatamente rilegati, creando così un piccolo angolo elegante e tranquillo, dove conversare di letteratura o godere comodamente della lettura.

The living room next to the library is just as elegant and luminous. Various sofas and two-colored armchairs next to the grand fireplace create a traditional and cozy setting.

Der neben der Bibliothek gelegene elegante Salon ist ein großer, heller Raum. Mehrere Sofas und zweifarbige Sessel gruppieren sich vor dem beeindruckenden Kamin – was dem Raum eine traditionelle Note verleiht. Dieser Platz läd ein zum gemütlichen Beisammensein.

Le salon, situé à côté de la bibliothèque, est également un espace élégant et lumineux. Il y a divers divans et fauteuils bicolores à côté de la grande cheminée – qui apporte une touche traditionnelle – créant ainsi un lieu de réunion accueillant.

El salón, situado junto a la biblioteca, es también un espacio elegante y luminoso. Se han dispuesto varios sofás y butacas bicolores al lado de la gran chimenea –que da un toque tradicional– y se ha creado así un acogedor lugar de reunión.

Anche il salone, accanto alla biblioteca, è uno spazio elegante e luminoso. Sono stati disposti vari divani e poltrone bicolori accanto al gran caminetto – che dà un tocco tradizionale – creando così un accogliente punto di ritrovo.

Colonial Air

□ This villa, surrounded by gardens, features a stylish, luxurious interior that lends a classic and elegant quality to the house. A relaxed and tranquil atmosphere presides everywhere, while on the porch, comfortable hammocks and several armchairs are an invitation to lay back and relax. Light and neutral tones predominate in the bedroom. The classical decoration of the main living area and dining room contrasts with the more rustic den, which displays hunting trophies, animal skins and a cane ceiling, which recall the home's original African culture and colonial influences.

□ Diese von Gärten umgebene Villa birgt luxuriös ausgestattete und geschmackvoll dekorierte Innenräume, die dem Haus einen klassischen, eleganten Touch verleihen. Überall herrscht eine entspannte, ruhige Atmosphäre. In der Loggia laden bequeme Liegestühle und einige Sessel zum Gespräch ein. In den Schlafräumen herrschen helle, neutrale Farben vor, die die Harmonie der Räume betonen. Die klassische Dekoration des Wohnzimmers und des Esszimmers steht im Kontrast zu einem ländlich gehaltenen kleineren Zimmer, in dem die afrikanische und koloniale Geschichte des Hauses mit Jagdtrophäen, Tierhäuten und einem Schilfdach zu Tage tritt.

□ Cette villa est entourée de jardins et possède des intérieurs luxueux au décor stylé qui confèrent à la maison un air classique et élégant. Toute l'habitation dégage une atmosphère décontractée et sereine. Dans l'atrium, des hamacs confortables et de nombreux sièges invitent à la conversation dans une ambiance détendue. Dans les chambres à coucher, les tons clairs et neutres prédominent, accentuant l'harmonie des pièces. La décoration classique du salon principal et de la salle à manger contraste avec celle de l'autre petit salon, plus rustique, où l'on découvre les origines africaines et coloniales de la villa par le biais des trophées de chasse, peaux d'animaux et toiture de roseaux.

□ Esta villa se encuentra rodeada de jardines y posee unos interiores lujosos y decorados con estilo, que dan un aire clásico y elegante a la casa. Se respira una atmósfera relajada y tranquila en toda la vivienda; en el porche, unas cómodas hamacas y varios sillones invitan a conversar relajadamente. Predominan en los dormitorios los tonos claros y neutros, que acentúan la armonía de las estancias. La decoración clásica del salón principal y del comedor contrasta con la de otro pequeño salón, más rústica, donde se descubren los orígenes africanos y coloniales de la villa a través de trofeos de caza, pieles de animales y una cubierta de caña.

□ Questa villa circondata da giardini possiede degli interni lussuosi e arredati con stile che danno un tocco classico ed elegante alla casa. In tutti i suoi vani si respira un'atmosfera distesa e tranquilla; nel porticato, delle comode amache e varie poltrone invitano a conversare rilassatamente. Nelle camere da letto predominano i toni chiari e neutri che accentuano l'armonia delle varie stanze. L'arredamento classico del salone principale e della sala da pranzo contrasta con quello più rustico di un altro saloncino, dove si scoprono le origini africane e coloniali della villa attraverso trofei di caccia, pelli di animali e una copertura di canna.

Location: **Cape Town, South Africa**
Interior design: **Julia Mordaunt**
Photographer: © **Andreas von Einsiedel**

Feature space: **Living room**

The spacious living room is decorated in light tones to enhance its luminosity. The curtains and upholstery lend warmth, while the classical furnishings and fireplace give it an atmosphere of grandeur.

Der weitläufige Salon ist in hellen Tönen gehalten, um ihm mehr Licht zu geben. Vorhänge und Bezüge lassen ihn behaglich und vornehm wirken, während die Möbel klassischen Zuschnitts und der Kamin dem Raum einen herrschaftlichen Charakter verleihen.

Le grand salon est décoré de tons clairs pour optimiser la luminosité. Rideaux et tapisseries dispensent chaleur et distinction, le style classique du mobilier et la cheminée confèrent un caractère seigneurial à la pièce.

El amplio salón está decorado con tonos claros para dar mayor luminosidad. Las cortinas y tapicerías proporcionan calidez y distinción, y el corte clásico del mobiliario y la chimenea confieren un carácter señorial a la estancia.

L'ampio salone è decorato in tonalità chiare per dare maggiore luminosità. Le tende e la tappezzeria rendono ancora più caldi e singolari l'ambiente, mentre il taglio classico dei mobili e il caminetto conferiscono un'aura di signorilità alla stanza.

The simple bedroom is void of any superfluous elements to maintain its peaceful atmosphere. Only the most essential furnishings are present, along with the use of light colors.

Das Schlafzimmer ist schlicht, ohne überflüssigen Schmuck eingerichtet, der die friedliche Atmosphäre stören könnte. Nur die nötigsten Möbelstücke sind vorhanden, und helle Farben herrschen vor.

La chambre à coucher est simple, sans éléments de décoration superflus qui puissent troubler l'atmosphère de paix. Le mobilier est réduit au minimum indispensable et les couleurs claires sont les protagonistes.

El dormitorio es sencillo, sin elementos decorativos superfluos que puedan perturbar la atmósfera de paz. El mobiliario es el mínimo indispensable y los colores claros son los protagonistas.

La camera da letto è semplice, priva di elementi decorativi superflui che possano perturbare la serena atmosfera di pace che vi si respira. I mobili sono ridotti al minimo indispensabile e a farla da protagonisti sono i colori chiari.

Indian Influences

☐ This property is situated on island-state of Mauritius, where the Indian and Urdu cultures are deeply rooted and clearly reflected in the interior decoration of the home. The broad windows and porches take advantage of the subtropical climate, and vegetation is present in practically all the areas of the home, turning the interior into a paradise for the senses. The tall ceilings and pointed arches accentuate the spaciousness of the rooms and white walls allow the valuable furniture pieces, tapestries and other decorative objects to stand out. The property, surrounded almost in its entirety by a wall, hides a large pool within its luscious gardens.

☐ Dieser Besitz liegt im Inselstaat Mauritius. Der allgemeine starke indisch-pakistanische Einfluss schlägt sich auch im Haus nieder, dessen große Fenster und Veranden dem subtropischen Klima angepasst sind. Überall ist das Grün der Vegetation präsent und lässt das Innere zu einem Fest der Sinne werden. Die hohen Decken und die Spitzbögen unterstreichen die Weite der Räume, während die weißen Wände die Qualität der Möbel, die wertvollen Bezugsstoffe und die anderen dekorativen Elemente dieses einzigartigen Wohnhauses hervorheben. Das Grundstück ist größtenteils von einer Mauer umgeben und birgt in den herrlichen Gärten unter anderem ein Schwimmbad.

☐ Dans cette ferme, située dans la République de Maurice, où les cultures indienne et urdu sont très enracinées, on ressent clairement l'influence hindoue. Les larges baies vitrées et atriums résultent du climat subtropical de la zone. La végétation est présente dans presque tous les coins convertissant l'intérieur en un paradis des sens. Les hauts plafonds et arcs outrepasses en ogive soulignent l'amplitude des pièces et le blanc des murs rehausse la qualité du mobilier, les tapis précieux et les autres éléments décoratifs qui ornent cette habitation particulière. La ferme, entourée en grande partie par un mur, occulte une grande piscine et des jardins magnifiques.

☐ En esta finca situada en la República de Mauricio, donde la cultura india y urdu están muy arraigadas, se percibe claramente la influencia hindú. Los amplios ventanales y porches se deben al clima subtropical de la zona. La vegetación está presente en casi todos los rincones y convierte el interior en un paraíso para los sentidos. Los altos techos y arcos de herradura apuntados acentúan la amplitud de las estancias, y el blanco de las paredes subraya la calidad del mobiliario, los preciosos tapices y el resto de los elementos decorativos que visten esta particular vivienda. La finca, rodeada en su mayor parte por un muro, esconde una gran piscina y unos magníficos jardines.

☐ In questa tenuta situata nella Republica di Mauritius, dove la cultura indiana e urdu sono molto radicate, si percepisce chiaramente l'influenza indù. Le grandi finestre e gli ampi porticati si devono al clima subtropicale della zona. La vegetazione, presente in quasi tutti gli angoli, trasforma gli interni della casa in un vero paradiso per i sensi. I soffitti alti e gli archi moreschi ogivali accentuano l'ampiezza delle stanze, e il bianco delle pareti sottolinea l'ottima fattura della mobilia, i pregiati arazzi e il resto degli elementi decorativi che abbelliscono questa singolare abitazione. La tenuta, circondata quasi interamente da un muro, nasconde una grande piscina e dei magnifici giardini.

Location: **Island-state of Mauritius**
Interior design: **Pierre Chaumard**
Photographer: © **Andreas von Einsiedel**

Feature space: **Patio, lounge area**

A small patio was transformed into a partially roofed lounge, ideal for chatting or sipping tea. Various rugs and cushions cover the floor, while a built bench decorated with plants borders the patio, that is open to the other areas of the home.

Ein kleiner Innenhof wurde zu einer teilweise überdachten Ruhezone umgestaltet, die zum Tee trinken und Plaudern einlädt. Der sich zu den anderen Räumen hin öffnende Hof ist von einer gemauerten Bank umgeben; Teppiche und Kissen bedecken den Boden, und die Pflanzen schaffen eine frische Atmosphäre.

Un petit patio a été transformé dans une zone de repos partiellement couverte, lieu idéal pour bavarder ou prendre un thé. Des tapis et des coussins recouvrent le sol et un banc ouvragé encadre le patio, ouvert sur d'autres pièces et orné de plantes qui rafraîchissent l'atmosphère.

Se ha transformado un pequeño patio en una zona de descanso parcialmente cubierta, un lugar ideal para charlar o para tomar un té. Varias alfombras y cojines cubren el suelo y un banco de obra rodea el patio, abierto a otras estancias y decorado con plantas que aportan frescura a la atmósfera.

Si è trasformato un piccolo cortile in una zona di riposo parzialmente coperta, un luogo ideale dove scambiare quattro chiacchiere o prendere un tè. Vari tappeti e cuscini coprono il pavimento e una panca in muratura circonda il cortile, aperto ad altre stanze e adornato con piante che rendono l'atmosfera ancora più fresca.

The climate of the island allows for a smooth transition between the home's interior and exterior, generating a sense of calm and serenity. A large porch opens onto the pool and provides intimate spaces for relaxation. An exterior dining area is located at one end of the porch from which the garden can be admired.

Das Klima der Insel ermöglicht die offene Bauweise des Hauses, das Ruhe und Gelassenheit ausstrahlt. Über eine großzügige Loggia, die vielfältige Ruhemöglichkeiten bietet, gelangt man zum Schwimmbad. An einem Ende der Loggia wurde ein Essplatz eingerichtet, von dem aus man die Gärten bewundern kann.

Le climat de l'île contribue à l'ouverture de l'habitation où l'on respire le calme et la sérénité. Un grand atrium donne sur la piscine et crée des espaces plus reclus pour s'y reposer. De même, une salle à manger extérieure a été installée à l'une des extrémités, d'où l'on peut contempler les jardins.

El clima de la isla contribuye a que la vivienda esté abierta y se respire en ella calma y serenidad. Un gran porche da a la piscina y proporciona espacios más recogidos en los que descansar. Asimismo, se ha ubicado un comedor exterior en uno de los extremos, desde donde se pueden contemplar los jardines.

Per via del clima dell'isola, le porte e le finestre delle stanze vengono lasciate aperte facendo impregnare l'abitazione di calma e serenità. Il grande porticato che dà alla piscina offre un ulteriore spazio di calma e tranquillità dove riposare. In una delle due estremità, è stata allestita una sorta di sala da pranzo esterna da dove è possibile ammirare i giardini.

The magnificent living area is one of the most luxurious rooms of the home. The furnishings and upholstery configure a comfortable interior, while the oriental motifs that adorn the tapestries are in harmony with the decoration's aesthetic style.

Der herrliche Salon ist einer der prächtigsten Räume des Hauses. Die Möbel und Bezugsstoffe machen ihn zu einem angenehmen Aufenthaltsort. Die orientalischen Motive der Teppiche an den Wänden harmonieren mit der Ästhetik der übrigen Einrichtung des Hauses.

Le magnifique salon est une des pièces les plus luxueuses de l'habitation. Le mobilier et les tapisseries forment un intérieur confortable, et les tapis aux motifs orientaux qui décorent les murs, rehaussent l'esthétique qui sublime toute la résidence.

El magnífico salón es una de las estancias más lujosas de la vivienda. El mobiliario y las tapicerías configuran un interior confortable, y las alfombras con motivos orientales que decoran las paredes están en armonía con la estética que inunda toda la residencia.

L'incantevole salotto è una delle stanze più lussuose dell'abitazione. I mobili e la tappezzeria foggiano degli interni confortevoli e i tappeti con motivi orientali che ornano le pareti confermano lo stile che permea tutta la dimora.

Calm and Exotism

☐ Light and simplicity define this residence situated on one of the beautiful islands of the Mediterranean. This generously-proportioned house boasts high ceilings and pure lines that create luminous spaces. The decorative objects from diverse parts of the world, such as drums, sculptures, and African-style decorative panels contribute warmth and contrast with the white interiors, skilfully combined with modern chairs and contemporary pieces of art. An interior and exterior pool, as well as a pond inside the patio, complete the look of this elegant contemporary home.

☐ Licht und Einfachheit kennzeichnen dieses Wohnhaus auf einer der schönsten Inseln des Mittelmeers. Das großzügige Haus hat hohe, helle, klare Räume, die in geraden Linien gestaltet und auf verschiedenen Ebenen angelegt sind. Dekorative Objekte aus aller Welt vermitteln Wärme und kontrastieren mit den weißen Wänden. Trommeln, Skulpturen und afrikanische Holztafeln werden geschickt mit modernen Stühlen und Werken zeitgenössischer Kunst kombiniert. Ein Schwimmbecken im Innen- und eins im Außenbereich sowie ein Wasserbecken im Patio ergänzen diese zeitgemäße, elegante Wohnanlage.

☐ Lumière et simplicité définissent cette résidence située dans une des plus belles îles de la Méditerranée. La maison, aux grandes dimensions, est dotée de très hauts plafonds et la pureté des lignes crée des pièces lumineuses et claires. Les objets de décoration d'origines diverses lui confèrent de la chaleur et contrastent avec les intérieurs blancs, articulés sur divers niveaux: tam-tams, sculptures et panneaux décoratifs de style africain se marient à merveille aux sièges modernes et aux œuvres d'art contemporain. Deux piscines, intérieure et extérieure ainsi que l'étang situé dans un patio parent cette demeure élégante et contemporaine.

☐ Luz y sencillez definen esta residencia situada en una de las más bellas islas del Mediterráneo. La casa, de grandes dimensiones, tiene los techos muy altos, y la pureza de las líneas crea estancias luminosas y claras. Los objetos de decoración de origen diverso aportan calidez y contrastan con el blanco de los interiores, articulados en varios niveles; tambores, esculturas y paneles decorativos de estilo africano combinan perfectamente con modernas sillas y obras de arte contemporáneo. Dos piscinas, una interior y otra exterior, y el estanque situado en un patio completan una vivienda elegante y contemporánea.

☐ Luce e semplicità definiscono questa dimora situata in una delle isole più belle del Mediterraneo. La casa, di grandi dimensioni, ha i soffitti molto alti, e la purezza delle linee crea ambienti chiari e luminosi. Gli oggetti decorativi di origine diversa apportano calore e contrastano con il bianco degli interni, articolati su diversi livelli; tamburi, sculture e pannelli decorativi di stile africano si abbinano perfettamente a sedie moderne e opere d'arte contemporanee. Due piscine, una interna e l'altra esterna, e il laghetto situato in un cortile completano un'abitazione elegante e contemporanea.

Location: Ibiza, Spain
Interior design: Bruno Raymond
Photographer: © Andreas von Einsiedel

Feature space: Main bedroom

The play on colors and textures of the main bedroom is present throughout the entire home. The grey floor and concrete bed along with the steel chairs, for example, contrast with a canoe on the headrest of the bed and the wooden panels of the dressing room.

Das Schlafzimmer der Besitzer ist ein Beispiel für das überall im Haus zu beobachtende Spiel der Farben und Texturen. Hier stehen das Grau des Bodens und die Stahlstühle im Kontrast mit dem Kanu am Kopfende des Bettes und den Holzpanelen im Ankleidezimmer.

La chambre de maîtres est un exemple du jeu de couleurs et de textures présentes dans la demeure. Par exemple, le gris du sol et du lit ouvragé ainsi que les fauteuils d'acier, contrastent avec un canoë situé à la tête du lit et les panneaux boisés du dressing.

El dormitorio principal es un ejemplo del juego de colores y texturas presente en toda la vivienda. Por ejemplo, el gris del suelo y la cama de obra, junto con los sillones de acero, contrastan con una canoa situada en la cabecera de la cama y con los paneles de madera del vestidor.

La camera da letto principale è un esempio del gioco di colori e texture presente in tutta l'abitazione. Ad esempio, il grigio del pavimento e il letto in muratura, assieme alle poltrone in acciaio, contrastano con una canoa posta sulla testata del letto e con i pannelli in legno dello spogliatoio.

The combination of textures is also present in the remaining areas of the home, including the main living room. The white table and large sofa contrast with the unique wooden stools, the zebra rug and the warm shades of the pillow covers.

Auch im Wohnzimmer trifft man wieder auf die Kombination verschiedener Texturen. Das Weiß der Tische und des riesigen Sofas kontrastiert mit dem Holz der originellen Hocker, dem Teppich im Zebramuster und den vielen Kissen mit Bezügen in warmen Farbtönen.

Ici à nouveau, le mélange de textures définie une des autres pièces principales : le salon. Le blanc des tables et de l'immense divan contraste avec le bois des tabourets originaux, le tapis imprimé de rayures et les tissus aux tons chauds des multiples coussins.

De nuevo una mezcla de texturas define otra de las estancias principales: el salón. El blanco de las mesas y del enorme sofá contrasta con la madera de los originales taburetes, la alfombra con estampado de cebra y las telas de tonos cálidos de los numerosos cojines.

Di nuovo un miscuglio di texture definisce un'altra delle stanze principali: il salone. Il bianco dei tavoli e dell'enorme sofà contrasta con il legno dei singolari sgabelli, il tappeto con stampato zebrato e le stoffe dai toni caldi dei numerosi cuscini.

Perfect Hosts

☐ This residence is located on Big Island, the largest of the Hawaii islands. The unusual entrance to the house consists of a wooden walkway that links the various pavilions that are surrounded by water, creating a fresh summer feel. The architecture and interior design are reminiscent of typical Hawaiian huts, enhanced with rich materials and decorative elements that magnify their elegance. The house opens onto the exterior via various terraces, pools and courtyards that allow with fabulous views of the ocean.

☐ Das Haus liegt auf Big Island, einer der Inseln des Hawaii-Archipels. Auffällig ist der Zugang zum Haus über einen hölzernen Steg, der die einzelnen Pavillons miteinander verbindet. Darunter fließt Wasser und erfrischt die Luft. Architektur und Einrichtung erinnern an die hawaiianischen Hütten, obwohl der einheimische Baustil hier mit wertvollen Materialien und dekorativen Elementen veredelt wurde. Das Haus öffnet sich nach draußen, sodass die bequem eingerichteten luxuriösen Zimmer sich über Terrassen, Schwimmbecken und Höfe mit dem Äußeren verbinden und atemberaubende Ausblicke auf den Ozean erlauben.

☐ Cette résidence est située sur Big Island, une des îles de l'archipel de Hawaï. L'accès, remarquable, à la maison se fait par une passerelle de bois qui unit les différents pavillons. L'eau circule entre eux, conférant une ambiance estivale rafraîchissante. L'architecture et la décoration rappellent les cabanes hawaïennes, mais ici réalisée avec des matériaux précieux et des éléments de décoration qui exaltent l'élégance du style. La maison s'ouvre sur l'extérieur, ce qui permet aux terrasses, piscines et patios d'être reliés aux pièces intérieures, luxueuses à souhait et confortable, tout en profitant des vues fabuleuses sur l'océan.

☐ Esta residencia está situada en Big Island, una de las islas del archipiélago de Hawai. Destaca la entrada a la casa, que se hace a través de una pasarela de madera que une los diferentes pabellones. El agua circula entre ellos y proporciona un ambiente estival refrescante. La arquitectura y la decoración recuerdan a las cabañas hawaianas, pero con ricos materiales y elementos decorativos que realzan la elegancia del estilo. La casa se abre al exterior, lo que permite que terrazas, piscinas y patios se relacionen con las estancias interiores, llenas de lujo y comodidad, mientras se disfruta de fabulosas vistas del océano.

☐ Questa residenza si trova a Big Island, una delle isole dell'arcipelago delle Hawai. Da notare l'accesso alla casa, che avviene mediante una passerella in legno che unisce i diversi padiglioni. L'acqua circola placida tra questi creando un ambiente estivo e rinfrescante. L'architettura e l'arredamento ricordano quelli delle capanne hawaiane, ma con materiali e oggetti di arredo che accentuano uno stile volutamente elegante. La casa si apre all'esterno mettendo in comunicazione i terrazzi, le piscine e i cortili con le stanze interne, piene di lusso e comodità, da dove è possibile godere delle favolose viste dell'oceano.

Location: **Big Island, Hawaii, USA**
Interior design: **Saint Dizier Design**
Photographer: © **Mary Nichols**

Feature space: **Bedrooms**

The bedrooms feature broad windows and exits. The wooden window-frames and furnishing create warm and elegant spaces. The furniture lends them a colonial atmosphere, rendered even more comfortable by the armchairs.

Die Schlafzimmer haben großzügige Fenster und Ausgänge nach draußen. Fensterrahmen und Möbel sind aus Holz, was die Behaglichkeit der Räume erhöht. Das Mobiliar schafft eine koloniale Atmosphäre, und die Sessel machen die Räume noch gemütlicher.

Les chambres à coucher de cette résidence disposent de larges baies vitrées et d'accès vers l'extérieur. Elles se caractérisent par l'emploi de bois pour les moulures et les meubles, qui confère chaleur et élégance à l'ensemble des pièces. Le mobilier crée une atmosphère coloniale et les sièges rendent les intérieurs encore plus confortables.

Los dormitorios de esta residencia tienen amplios ventanales y salidas al exterior, y se caracterizan por el empleo de madera en molduras y muebles, lo que aporta calidez y elegancia a las estancias. El mobiliario crea una atmósfera colonial y los sillones hacen aún más confortables los interiores.

Le camere da letto di questa casa presentano grandi finestre e uscite verso l'esterno e si caratterizzano per l'impiego del legno nelle modanature e nei mobili dai toni caldi e la spiccata eleganza. Negli interni, accanto a delle comode poltrone, campeggia una mobilia di stile coloniale.

The interiors are decorated with furniture and objects that radiate extravagance and luxury. This house with its comfortable interior and exterior rooms is the perfect place in which to relax and rest.

Die Innenräume sind mit Möbeln und Gegenständen eingerichtet, die Pracht und Luxus ausstrahlen. Das Haus mit seinen bequemen Salons im Innen- und Außenbereich ist der ideale Ort, um sich auszuruhen und zu entspannen.

Les intérieurs de la résidence sont parés de meubles et objets qui exaltent la splendeur et le luxe. La maison est un lieu idéal pour se détendre et se reposer, vu que tant à l'intérieur qu'à l'extérieur, il est possible de profiter du confort de divers salons.

Los interiores de la residencia están decorados con muebles y objetos que acentúan la suntuosidad y el lujo. La casa es un lugar perfecto para relajarse y descansar, ya que, tanto en el interior como en el exterior, se puede disfrutar de confortables salones.

Gli interni della dimora sono arredati con mobili ed oggetti che accentuano la sontuosità e il lusso. Questa casa è il luogo ideale dove rilassarsi e riposare, sia all'interno che all'esterno, grazie a dei raffinati e confortevoli saloni.

Retreat in a Fishing Village

☐ This luxurious residence located on the coast of the island of Majorca presents a successful mixture of styles. The vaulted ceiling was renovated and terrazzo tiles were laid on the floor. Inside, the rural atmosphere was maintained by exposing the stone structure. The furniture and decorative objects originate from diverse places: Buddha busts and Asian parasols coexist with rustic tables and chairs. Restored doors adorn the vestibule, one of the bedrooms and the dining room adding an air of uniqueness and distinction.

☐ Dieses luxuriöse Anwesen an der mallorquinischen Küste ist eine gelungene Mischung verschiedener Stile. Die gewölbte Decke wurde restauriert und der Boden mit Terrazzofliesen ausgelegt. In den Zimmern wurde der Stein der Mauern unverputzt gelassen, um den rustikalen Charakter zu unterstreichen. Möbel und dekorative Objekte stammen von den verschiedensten Orten: Buddhas und orientalische Schirme behaupten sich neben bäuerlichen Tischen und Stühlen. Für den Eingang, eines der Schlafzimmer und das Esszimmer wurden alte Türen hergerichtet, die den Räumen einen ausgefallenen Touch verleihen.

☐ Cette résidence luxueuse, située sur la côte de l'île de Majorque, offre un mélange réussi des styles. Le plafond d'entrevous a été restauré et le sol revêtu de dalles de granit. A l'intérieur des pièces, la pierre a été laissée apparente pour rehausser le caractère rural. Le mobilier et les objets de décoration proviennent de différents endroits : têtes de bouddhas et ombrelles orientales côtoient tables et sièges rustiques. Des portes récupérées décorent le vestibule, une des chambres et la salle à manger, leur conférant ainsi une touche de distinction et d'originalité.

☐ Esta lujosa residencia situada en la costa de la isla de Mallorca es una acertada mezcla de estilos. Se ha reformado el techo de bovedillas y se han colocado en el suelo unas baldosas de terrazo. En el interior de las estancias, se ha dejado a la vista la piedra para realzar la atmósfera rural. El mobiliario y los objetos de decoración provienen de diferentes lugares: cabezas de budas y sombrillas orientales conviven con mesas y sillas de estilo rústico. Unas puertas recuperadas decoran el recibidor, uno de los dormitorios y el comedor, y les dan un toque de distinción y originalidad.

☐ Questa lussuosa residenza situata nella costa dell'isola di Maiorca è un miscuglio ben riuscito di stili diversi. Si è ristrutturato il soffitto a voltini e per terra è stato collocato un tipico pavimento alla veneziana. All'interno delle stanze, al fine di accentuare ulteriormente l'atmosfera rurale, la pietra dei muri è stata lasciata a vista. I mobili e gli oggetti di ornamento provengono da luoghi diversi: teste di Budda e ombrellini orientali convivono con tavoli e sedie in stile rustico. Delle porte restaurate decorano l'ingresso, una delle camere da letto e la sala da pranzo, dando a questi ambienti un tocco di distinzione e originalità.

Location: **Majorca, Spain**
Interior design: **Niels Hansen**
Photographer: © **Andreas von Einsiedel**

Feature space: **Den**

The master bedroom, although not very big, has a warm and tranquil atmosphere. The earth shades of the walls combine perfectly with the canopy bed and furnishings, creating a warm and intimate space.

Das Schlafzimmer ist zwar nicht sehr groß, besitzt aber eine warme, beruhigende Atmosphere. Die Erdtöne der Wände harmonieren perfekt mit dem Himmelbett und den Möbeln und schaffen einen intimen Privatbereich.

La chambre de maîtres n'est pas très grande. Toutefois, l'ambiance y est chaleureuse et calme. Les tons ocres des murs s'harmonisent à la perfection avec le lit à baldaquin et le mobilier, créant un espace intime et privé.

El dormitorio principal no es de grandes dimensiones; sin embargo, la atmósfera es cálida y tranquila. Los tonos tierra de las paredes combinan a la perfección con la cama con dosel y con el mobiliario y crean un espacio íntimo y privado.

Nella camera da letto principale, pur non essendo eccessivamente grande, si respira un'atmosfera accogliente e tranquilla. I toni terra delle pareti si abbinano alla perfezione con il letto col baldacchino e la mobilia, creando uno spazio intimo e privato.

A small den is linked to the master bedroom and combines a variety of styles with an eclectic and charming effect. The furniture consists of a leather pouf as a center table, a study and two small obelisks.

Ein kleines Wohnzimmer schließt sich an das Schlafzimmer an. Die Einrichtung, bestehend aus einem Puff als Couchtisch, einem Sekretär und zwei kleinen Obelisken, fügt sich zu einer harmonischen Einheit zusammen.

Un petit salon communique avec la chambre de maîtres et mélange des styles différents au sein d'un espace éclectique et ravissant. Le mobilier, un pouf en cuir en guise de table centrale, un secrétaire et deux petits obélisques, forment un ensemble harmonieux.

Un pequeño salón comunica con el dormitorio principal y mezcla varios estilos diferentes en un espacio ecléctico y encantador. El mobiliario, un puf de piel como mesa de centro, un secreter y dos pequeños obeliscos, forma un conjunto armónico.

Un piccolo salone, comunicante con la camera da letto principale, mescola stili diversi in uno spazio eclettico e incantevole. L'arredamento, costituito da un puff di pelle che funge da tavolino d'appoggio, un secretaire e due piccoli obelischi, forma un complesso armonico.

Elegance in the Alps

☐ For the owner of this villa in the French Alps, this place is a refuge filled with a multitude of childhood memories. The architectural style of the exterior is typical of the region. Upon refurbishing, however, the interior did not maintain any rustic elements, but created simple and clear rooms. The furniture, lamps and fabrics were carefully chosen to generate an extremely elegant ambience. All of the objects are original works that are discreetly integrated into the existing decor. Most remarkable is the personal touch of the bedrooms and the wall around the fireplace, finished in a striking silver color.

☐ Dieses Chalet in den französischen Alpen ist für seine Besitzerin ein mit Kindheitserinnerungen erfüllter Rückzugsort. Von außen betrachtet handelt es sich um ein Haus im für diese Region typischen Baustil. Im Inneren sollten aber keine rustikalen Elemente erhalten bleiben, sondern schlichte, klare Räume entstehen. Möbel, Lampen und Stoffe wurden sorgfältig ausgewählt, um ein Ambiente von äußerster Eleganz zu schaffen. Alle Stücke sind Originale, die sich unauffällig mit der übrigen Einrichtung verbinden. Hervorzuheben sind die individuell gestalteten Schlafzimmer und die überraschende silberne Wand, die den Kamin umgibt.

☐ Pour la propriétaire de ce chalet dans les Alpes françaises, ce lieu est un refuge qui évoque une multitude de souvenirs d'enfance. De l'extérieur, on aperçoit une construction dont l'architecture semble typique de la région. La condition préalable de ne pas mettre en valeur les éléments rustiques, confère une atmosphère sobre et pure. Le mobilier, les lampes et les tissus ont été soigneusement sélectionnés pour créer une ambiance d'une élégance extrême. Toutes les pièces de la demeure sont originales, mais discrètes, et en harmonie avec le reste de la décoration. A l'intérieur, on remarque les chambres à coucher personnalisées. Le mur qui entoure la cheminée étonne par sa couleur argentée.

☐ Para la propietaria de este chalé en los Alpes franceses, este lugar es un refugio que evoca multitud de recuerdos de su infancia. Desde el exterior, se percibe como una construcción con la arquitectura típica de la región. La condición previa de no destacar ningún elemento rústico propicia una atmósfera sencilla y clara. El mobiliario, las lámparas y las telas han sido cuidadosamente escogidas para crear un ambiente de extrema elegancia. Todas las piezas en la vivienda son originales, pero discretas, y combinan con el resto de la decoración. En el interior destacan los dormitorios personalizados y la pared que rodea la chimenea, de un sorprendente color plateado.

☐ Per la proprietaria di questo chalet nelle Alpi francesi, questo posto costituisce un rifugio che evoca molti ricordi d'infanzia. Dall'esterno, si percepisce come una costruzione caratterizzata dall'architettura tipica della regione. L'intenzione iniziale di non mettere in risalto nessun elemento rustico propizia un'atmosfera semplice e lineare. La mobilia, le lampade e le stoffe sono state scelte con la massima cura al fine di creare un ambiente di estrema eleganza. Tutti i pezzi che adornano l'abitazione sono originali, ma discreti, e si abbinano al resto degli elementi di arredo. All'interno una menzione speciale spetta alle camere da letto e alla parete che circonda il camino, di un sorprendente color argentato.

Location: **Megève, France**
Interior design: **Carlo Rampazzi**
Photographer: © **Reto Guntli / Zapaimages**

Feature space: **Living room**

The original furnishings and silver-colored fireplace are the dominating elements of the living area. The room is unique and at the same time discreet and sophisticated. The warmth of the fabrics and the soft tone of the walls make for a remarkably elegant ambience.

Die ausgesuchten Möbelstücke und der silberne Kamin bestimmen den Gesamteindruck des Wohnzimmers. Entstanden ist ein origineller und dabei diskreter Raum mit viel Klasse. Die Wärme der Stoffe und der zarte Farbton der Wände kreieren ein ausgesuchtes Ambiente.

Le mobilier original et la cheminée, argentée, sont les deux éléments qui se détachent le plus du salon. L'espace obtenu est unique, tout en restant discret et distingué. La chaleur des tissus et la douceur du ton des murs créent une ambiance élégante et sophistiquée.

El original mobiliario y la chimenea, de color plateado, son los dos elementos que más destacan del salón. Se ha conseguido un espacio único, pero al mismo tiempo discreto y con clase. La calidez de las telas y el tono suave de las paredes crean un ambiente elegante y sofisticado.

L'originale mobilia e il caminetto, in colore argentato, sono gli elementi che colpiscono di più l'attenzione in questo salone. Si è riusciti ad ottenere uno spazio unico, ma al contempo discreto e con classe. I toni caldi delle stoffe e quelli tenui delle pareti creano un ambiente elegante e sofisticato.

Villa Salina

☐ This attractive villa located in the Aeolian Islands dates back to the year 1700 and was originally a malvasia wine-producing farm. Its restoration aimed to preserve the local architectural style and at the same time, add a modern air. The distribution of the interior spaces, organized around a central patio, was maintained and typical elements such as the Sicilian terracotta tiles were recovered. The white color enhances the purity of the lines and the decoration creates delicate and luminous rooms adorned with ethnic rugs and Arabic decorative objects.

☐ Diese attraktive Villa liegt auf den Äolischen Inseln. Sie stammt aus dem Jahre 1700 und war ursprünglich ein Weingut, auf dem Malvasiertrauben verarbeitet wurden. Bei der Umgestaltung sollte trotz Modernisierung die typische Architektur der Region erhalten bleiben. Die Anordnung der Räumlichkeiten um einen Innenhof wurde nicht verändert. Ausgewählte Elemente, wie die sizilianischen Terrakottafliesen, wurden restauriert. Die weiße Farbe unterstreicht die Klarheit der Linien; die Dekoration lässt geschmackvolle, helle Räume entstehen, die mit Teppichen mit Ethno-Motiven und mit dekorativen Objekten arabischer Herkunft ausgestattet sind.

☐ Cette belle villa se trouve sur les Iles Eoliques. La maison, datant de 1700, était à l'origine une ferme ou l'on fabriquait le vin de malvoisie. La restauration devait garder l'esprit de l'architecture de la région et apporter, en même temps, une touche moderne. La distribution des pièces a été conservée autour d'un patio central en récupérant des éléments typiques comme les dalles de terracota sicilienne. Le blanc exalte la pureté des lignes et la décoration crée des atmosphères subtiles et lumineuses, ornées de tapis ethniques et d'objets décoratifs arabes.

☐ Esta atractiva villa se encuentra en las islas Eolias. La casa data de 1700 y era originalmente una granja donde se fabricaba vino de malvasía. La rehabilitación tenía el objetivo de conservar el espíritu de la arquitectura de la zona y aportar, al mismo tiempo, un matiz moderno. Se ha mantenido la distribución de las estancias alrededor de un patio central y se han recuperado elementos típicos, como las baldosas de terracota siciliana. El color blanco realza la pureza de las líneas y la decoración crea ambientes delicados y luminosos, adornados con alfombras de motivos tribales y objetos de decoración árabes.

☐ Questa affascinante villa si trova nell'arcipelago delle Isole Eolie. La casa, all'epoca una tenuta dove si produceva vino Malvasia, risale al 1700. I lavori di ristrutturazione avevano come obiettivo conservare lo spirito dell'architettura della zona e dare allo stesso tempo un tocco di modernità. La distribuzione delle stanze, attorno a un cortile centrale, non è stata alterata e si sono recuperati elementi tipici come le piastrelle in terracotta siciliana. Il bianco mette il risalto la purezza delle linee e l'arredamento crea ambienti delicati e luminosi, adornati con tappeti dagli stampati tribali e oggetti decorativi arabi.

Location: **Aeolian Islands, Italy**
Architect: **Prima Design**
Photographer: © **Giorgio Baroni**

Feature space: **Sheltered terrace**

The bedrooms are situated around the terrace sheltered by a reed-covered roof, which constitutes the center of family social life. Cushions adorned with tribal motifs and Arabic lamps enhance the charm and delicacy of the space. The villa provides the owners with the perfect balance to city life.

Die Zimmer sind um eine Terrasse herum angeordnet, die das Zentrum des Familienlebens darstellt und von einem Schilfrohrdach vor der Sonne geschützt wird. Kissen mit folkloristischen Motiven und arabische Lampen unterstreichen die Anmut dieses Ortes. Für die Bewohner ist die Villa der Gegenpol zum Leben in der Stadt.

Les pièces sont disposées autour de la terrasse, centre de la vie sociale de la famille, et une toiture de bambous protège du soleil pendant la journée. Des coussins aux motifs ethniques et les lampes arabes exaltent la grâce et la délicatesse de l'espace. Pour les propriétaires, la villa est la parfaite antidote à la vie citadine.

Las habitaciones están dispuestas alrededor de la terraza, centro de la vida social de la familia, y una cubierta de cañas protege del sol durante el día. Unos cojines con motivos tribales y las lámparas árabes realzan la gracia y delicadeza del espacio. Para los propietarios, la villa es el antídoto perfecto para la vida de la ciudad.

Le stanze sono disposte attorno al cortile esterno, vero centro della vita sociale della famiglia, coperto da un graticcio di canne che durante il giorno protegge dal sole. Alcuni cuscini con motivi tribali e le lampade arabe accentuano il fascino e la delicatezza dell'ambiente. Per i proprietari, l'atmosfera tranquilla della villa è l'antidoto perfetto alla frenetica vita della città.

The location is one of this residence's greatest attractions. The surroundings lend the villa calm and tranquility, converting it into a refuge amidst the mountains with a spectacular view of the sea.

Die Lage dieses Hauses ist eine seiner größten Attraktionen. Die Umgebung schirmt die Villa ab, ruhig und ungestört verwandelt sie sich zu einem Refugium in den Bergen mit einer spektakulären Aussicht auf das Meer.

La situation de cette pièce est un de ses attraits. L'environnement confère calme et tranquillité à la maison qui s'élève entre les montagnes, à l'instar d'un magnifique refuge isolé avec vues sur la mer.

La ubicación de esta vivienda es uno de sus atractivos. El entorno impregna de calma y tranquilidad la casa, que se levanta entre las montañas como un magnífico refugio aislado con vistas al mar.

Indubbiamente la posizione di questa abitazione è una delle sue attrattive principali. L'ambiente impregna di calma e tranquillità la casa, che si erge tra le montagne come un imponente rifugio isolato con magnifiche viste sul mare.

The kitchen is furnished with pieces designed by the architect, adapting perfectly to the traditional style of the farm. The modern elements within the home do not disturb the traditional and delicate atmosphere that presides in the villa.

In der Küche trifft man auf einige Möbelstücke, die vom Architekten entworfen wurden und sich perfekt an den traditionellen Stil des früheren Weingutes anpassen. Keines der modernen Elemente stört die überall herrschende zauberhafte Atmosphäre vergangener Zeiten.

Dans la cuisine, certains meubles dessinés par l'architecte, s'adaptent à merveille au style traditionnel de l'ancienne ferme. Aucun des éléments modernes présents dans la demeure ne vient rompre l'atmosphère emprunte de tradition et de subtilité qui s'y dégage.

En la cocina se encuentran algunas piezas de mobiliario diseñadas por el arquitecto, que se adaptan a la perfección al estilo tradicional de la antigua granja. Ninguno de los elementos modernos presentes en la vivienda rompen la atmósfera de tradición y delicadeza que se respira en ella.

In cucina si trovano alcuni pezzi di mobili disegnati dall'architetto che si adattano alla perfezione allo stile tradizionale dell'antica tenuta. Nessuno degli elementi moderni presenti nell'abitazione spezza l'atmosfera di tradizione e delicatezza che vi si respira.

Terrestrial Paradise

□ Originally conceived as a summer residence, this house incorporates elements typical of Indonesian architecture; the main pavilion, for example is connected to the remaining areas by various walkways. An extraordinary mixture of eastern and western styles results in an imaginative, exotic and stylish atmosphere. The living room ceiling, open to the exterior, was constructed with local materials and teakwood pillars that support the structure. The extreme elegance of the villa is also reflected in the pool, gardens and the variety of styles present in the decor. Living here is perhaps the closest thing to living in paradise.

□ Dieses Haus wurde ursprünglich als Sommerresidenz errichtet und vereint typische Merkmale indonesischer Architektur: So ist z.B. der Hauptpavillon über Stege mit den anderen Teilen verbunden. Aus einer außergewöhnlichen Mischung westlicher und östlicher Stile ist eine fantasievolle, exotische Wohnung mit ausgeprägtem Eigencharakter entstanden. Die Decke des nach außen offenen Salons besteht aus einheimischen Materialien, die Struktur wird von Teakholzpfeilern getragen. Die ausgesuchte Eleganz der Anlage zeigt sich auch beim Schwimmbecken, in den Gärten und in der stilistischen Vielfalt der Einrichtung – wer hier wohnt, fühlt sich wie im Paradies.

□ Conçue à l'origine comme une résidence d'été, cette demeure réunit des éléments typiques de l'architecture indonésienne : le pavillon principal, par exemple, communique avec le reste grâce à des passerelles. On observe un extraordinaire mélange de styles orientaux et occidentaux sublimés pour créer une demeure imaginaire, exotique, de grand style. Le toit du salon, ouvert vers l'extérieur, est construit en matériaux locaux, avec des piliers de bois de teck pour soutenir sa structure. L'extrême élégance de cette villa se reflète aussi dans la piscine, les jardins et la variété des styles de la décoration : vivre dans cette résidence, c'est comme être au paradis.

□ Ideada originalmente como residencia estival, esta vivienda reúne elementos típicos de la arquitectura de Indonesia; el pabellón principal, por ejemplo, se comunica con el resto a través de pasarelas. Se observa una extraordinaria mezcla de estilos oriental y occidental cuyo resultado es una vivienda imaginativa, exótica y con gran estilo. El techo del salón, abierto al exterior, se ha construido con materiales propios del lugar y pilares de madera de teca que soportan su estructura. La extrema elegancia de esta villa se refleja también en la piscina, en los jardines y en la variedad de estilos que presenta la decoración; vivir en esta residencia es como estar en el paraíso.

□ Ideata originariamente come una casa di villeggiatura, questa abitazione raggruppa elementi tipici dell'architettura dell'Indonesia; il padiglione principale, per esempio, comunica con il resto attraverso delle passerelle. Si osserva una straordinaria mescolanza tra stile orientale ed occidentale il cui risultato è un'abitazione immaginativa, esotica e davvero elegante. Il soffitto del salone, aperto all'esterno, è stato costruito con materiali del posto e pilastri in legno di tek che sorreggono la struttura. L'enorme eleganza di questa villa si rispecchia pure nella piscina, nei giardini e nella varietà di stili che presenta l'arredamento; vivere in questa dimora è quasi come stare in paradiso.

Location: **Bali, Indonesia**
Architect: **Antonio Ismael/Triaco Design, Cheong Yukuan**
Photographer: **© Reto Guntli/Zapaimages**

Feature space: **Living room**

The main living room is an exuberant and majestic space with various lounge areas, some of which face and the pool area. The ceiling is an example of typical Balinese architecture, and features furniture made of rattan as well as batik cushions of different size.

Der Hauptsalon ist ein überwältigender, prachtvoller Raum mit verschiedenen Ruhezonen, von denen einige sich nach draußen bzw. zum Schwimmbad orientieren. Das Dach ist ein Beispiel typischer balinesischer Baukunst. In der Ausstattung fallen die Rattanmöbel und die Kissen verschiedener Größe mit Batiken ins Auge.

Le salon principal est une pièce exubérante et majestueuse, déclinant plusieurs zones de repos, dont certaines donnent sur l'extérieur et vers la piscine. Le toit est un exemple de l'architecture typique de Bali. La décoration fait ressortir les meubles de rotin, ainsi que les coussins et édredons en batik.

El salón principal es una exuberante y majestuosa estancia con varias zonas de descanso, algunas de las cuales dan al exterior y a la piscina. El techo es un ejemplo de la arquitectura típica de Bali y en la decoración destacan los muebles de ratán, así como los cojines de tela batik de tamaños diferentes.

Il salone principale è formato da un ambiente esuberante e maestoso con varie zone di riposo, alcune delle quali danno all'esterno e alla piscina. Il soffitto è un esempio dell'architettura tipica di Bali; tra i pezzi di arredo, colpiscono l'occhio i mobili in ratan così come i cuscini, di varie dimensioni, in tela Batik.

The guest pavilions are decorated in a more modern and contemporary style, while maintaining the elegance of the main residence. Designed in a more minimalist style, this room also incorporates references to the local culture, such as the small wooden boxes that form part of the decoration.

Die Gästepavillons folgen einem modernen, zeitgenössischen Entwurf, ohne auf die Eleganz des Hauptpavillons zu verzichten. Obwohl dieser Raum minimalistisch eingerichtet ist, sind die Reminiszenzen an die lokale Kultur nicht zu übersehen, wie etwa die kleinen Holzkistchen, die zur Dekoration gehören.

Les pavillons pour invités suivent une esthétique plus moderne et contemporaine, même s'ils affichent l'élégance de la résidence principale. Cette pièce est plus minimaliste, mais les références à la culture locale sont visibles, à l'instar des petites boites en bois qui font partie de la décoration.

Los pabellones para invitados siguen una estética más moderna y contemporánea, aunque poseen toda la elegancia de la residencia principal. Esta estancia es más minimalista, pero aun así se perciben referencias a la cultura local en las pequeñas cajas de madera que forman parte de la decoración.

I padiglioni per gli ospiti seguono un'estetica più moderna e attuale, sebbene possiedano tutta l'eleganza della residenza principale. Pur essendo più minimalista, in questa stanza sono evidenti alcuni riferimenti alla cultura locale, come le piccole scatole in legno che decorano l'ambiente.

Residence in Pasadena

☐ This house is an excellent example of the Spanish colonial style of southern California. Built between 1915 and 1918, it is part of what was originally a large villa that was later subdivided. After being remodeled several times over the years, the owners decided to recover its original spirit. New rooms were added and various spaces were restored, including the entrance hall and the living room, which features a grand fireplace. The garden and exterior architecture form a wonderful unit full of harmony, enchanting to marvel the visitor. The elegant and exclusive materials used in the décor accentuate the beauty of the interiors.

☐ Dieses zwischen 1915 und 1918 errichtete Haus ist ein hervorragendes Beispiel für den spanischen Kolonialstil im Süden Kaliforniens. Es ist ein Teil eines größeren Besitzes, der später geteilt wurde. Im Laufe der Jahre wurde das Haus mehrfach umgebaut, bis die jetzigen Besitzer sich entschlossen, den ursprünglichen Charakter wiederherzustellen. Die Eingangshalle und der Salon mit seinem mächtigen Kamin wurden restauriert, andere Räume neu eingerichtet. Die Gärten und die Außenansicht ergeben ein harmonisches Ganzes, dass geeignet ist den Besucher zu bezaubern. Die Schönheit der Innenräume wird von den bei der Einrichtung verwendeten edlen Materialien besonders unterstrichen.

☐ Cette maison est un excellent exemple de style colonial espagnol du sud de la Californie. Construite entre 1915 et 1918, est la maison une partie de la ferme d'origine qui a été ultérieurement divisée. Au fil des années, elle a subit diverses restaurations jusqu'à ce que les derniers propriétaires aient décidé de récupérer l'esprit initial. Le vestibule a été restauré ainsi que le salon d'où se détache une grande cheminée, et de nouveaux espaces ont été crées. Les jardins et l'architecture extérieure forment un fabuleux ensemble très harmonieux, conçu pour le plaisir du visiteur. Les élégants et nobles matériaux utilisés pour la décoration subliment la beauté des intérieurs.

☐ Esta casa es una excelente muestra del estilo colonial español del sur de California; construida entre 1915 y 1918, es una parte de la finca original que fue posteriormente subdividida. A lo largo de los años, se realizaron diversas remodelaciones en la vivienda hasta que los últimos propietarios decidieron recuperar el espíritu original. Se han rehabilitado el vestíbulo y el salón, donde destaca una gran chimenea, y se han creado nuevos espacios. Los jardines y la arquitectura exterior forman un fabuloso conjunto lleno de armonía, pensado para deleitar al visitante. Los elegantes y nobles materiales utilizados en la decoración acentúan la belleza de los interiores.

☐ Questa casa rappresenta un magnifico esempio dello stile coloniale spagnolo del sud della California; edificata tra il 1915 e il 1918, è solo una parte della tenuta originale che è stata successivamente suddivisa. Nel corso degli anni, l'abitazione è stata soggetta a diverse ristrutturazioni fino a che gli ultimi proprietari decisero di recuperarne lo spirito originario. I lavori di restauro hanno interessato l'atrio e il salone, dove spicca un grande camino, e hanno permesso la creazione di nuovi spazi. I giardini e l'architettura esterna formano un tutt'uno favoloso pieno di armonia, specialmente pensato per piacere al visitatore. I materiali, eleganti e nobili, adoperati per arredare la casa accentuano la bellezza degli interni.

Location: **Pasadena, California, USA**
Architect: **KAA Design Group**
Interior design: **Chris Barrett Design**
Photographer: **© Pizzi and Thompson**

Feature space: **Living room**

The grand living room is one of the recovered spaces within the home, and features a large fireplace that exemplifies the Spanish colonial style as well as a ceiling with elaborate moldings. Comfortable sofas, elegant furnishings and lavish fabrics convey a feeling of calm and opulence.

Das große Wohnzimmer gehört zu den wiederhergestellten Räumen. Hier fallen der große Kamin und die hölzerne Kassettendecke ins Auge, die typisch für den spanischen Kolonialstil sind. Bequeme Sofas, elegante Möbel und ausgesuchte Stoffe vermitteln ein Gefühl von Ruhe und Opulenz.

La grande salle est une des pièces récupérées. On y remarque une grande cheminée qui exalte le style colonial espagnol et un plafond à caissons boisés. Des divans confortables, un mobilier élégant et des tissus riches diffusent un mélange de calme et d'opulence.

La gran sala es una de las estancias recuperadas; destaca una gran chimenea que acentúa el estilo colonial español y un techo con artesones de madera. Confortables sofás, un mobiliario elegante y unas telas ricas transmiten una mezcla de calma y opulencia.

La grande sala è una delle stanze che sono state recuperate; vi campeggia un grande camino che sottolinea lo stile coloniale spagnolo e un soffitto a cassettoni. Comodi divani, mobili raffinati e stoffe pregiate trasmettono una sensazione congiunta di calma ed opulenza.

The main bathroom is fashioned in a distinctly Arabic style, featuring bright blue tiles, pointed arches and a bathtub situated under a wooden canopy. The lamps and the geometric and colorful mosaic design complete the decoration of this room.

Das Badezimmer ist einem ausgeprägt arabischen Stil gestaltet worden: mit leuchtend blauen Azulejos-Fliesen, Spitzbögen und einer Badewanne unter einem hölzernen Baldachin. Die Lampen und das Mosaik mit dem bunten geometrischen Muster vervollständigen das Ensemble.

La salle de bains principale est décorée d'une frise de style arabe, d'azulejos bleu vif, d'arcs en lancette et d'une baignoire située sous un baldaquin en bois. Les lampes et la mosaïque aux dessins géométriques et coloristes parachèvent l'ensemble.

El baño principal está decorado con un marcado estilo árabe, con azulejos de color azul brillante, arcos apuntados y una bañera situada bajo un baldaquino de madera. Las lámparas y el mosaico de diseño geométrico y colorista completan el conjunto.

Il bagno principale è decorato in uno spiccato stile arabo, con piastrelle smaltate di colore azzurro brillante, archi ogivali e una vasca situata sotto un baldacchino in legno. Completano il tutto le lampade e il mosaico dai disegni geometrici e coloristici.

Villa Fiesole

☐ Despite its 16th century style facade, this villa near Florence was in fact built in the 14th century. The structure underwent a constant series of renovations: the pool was constructed in 1732, and the interior was entirely remodeled in the 18th century. Adelaide of Savoy was one of its illustrious tenants, and today the villa belongs to an Italian family that has dedicated much time and effort to its restoration. The floors, moldings and murals have been preserved, and its classical and extravagant decoration is well-suited to its historical context. Outside, a porch leads to the well-preserved gardens.

☐ Diese Villa befindet sich in der Nähe von Florenz und wurde im 14. Jh. errichtet, doch die Fassade wurde im Geschmack des 16. Jh umgestaltet. Das Haus wurde vielfach umgebaut: 1732 wurde das Wasserbecken angelegt, und im 18. Jh. wurde das gesamte Innere erneuert. Unter den berühmten Besitzern ist Adelaide von Savoyen hervorzuheben. Heute gehört die Villa einer italienischen Familie, die viel Zeit und Mühe in die Restaurierung investiert hat. Aus der Entstehungszeit erhalten geblieben sind die Fußböden, die Stuckleisten an den Decken und die Wandmalereien. Die Ausstattung ist klassisch zu nennen, das prächtige Mobiliar passt hervorragend in die Räume. Draußen führt eine Loggia zu den gut erhaltenen Gärten.

☐ Cette ville située près de Florence a été construite au XIVe siècle, bien que sa façade suive le goût architectural du XVIe siècle. Elle a été constamment remaniée : en 1732, la piscine a été construite et au XVIIIe siècle, tout l'intérieur a été entièrement remodelé. Parmi ses illustres propriétaires, on cite Adélaïde de Savoie. Actuellement, elle appartient à une famille italienne qui a consacré du temps et des efforts à la restaurer. Le carrelage, les moulures et les peintures murales ont été conservées. La décoration classique et le somptueux mobilier se marient à merveille à l'intérieur de la résidence. A l'extérieur, un atrium conduit aux jardins, soigneusement entretenus.

☐ Esta villa situada cerca de Florencia fue construida en el siglo XIV, aunque su fachada sigue el gusto arquitectónico del siglo XVI. Las remodelaciones han sido constantes: en 1732 se construyó la piscina y en el siglo XVIII se remodeló prácticamente todo el interior. Entre sus ilustres propietarios se encuentra Adelaida de Saboya. En la actualidad, pertenece a una familia italiana que ha dedicado tiempo y esfuerzo en su restauración. Se han conservado el pavimento, las molduras y las pinturas murales; la decoración es clásica y el suntuoso mobiliario combina a la perfección con el interior de la residencia. En el exterior, un porche conduce a los jardines, cuidadosamente conservados.

☐ Sebbene la sua facciata segua un gusto architettonico cinquecentesco, questa villa nei pressi di Firenze è stata costruita nel XIV secolo. Le ristrutturazioni sono state costanti: nel 1732 fu costruita la piscina e più avanti sono stati restaurati praticamente tutti gli interni. Tra i suoi illustri proprietari, la villa annovera anche Adelaide di Savoia. Attualmente, appartiene ad una famiglia italiana che ha dedicato sforzi e tempo alla sua completa ristrutturazione. Tra gli elementi che si sono mantenuti tali, le modanature e i dipinti murali; l'arredamento è classico e il suntuoso mobilio combina alla perfezione con gli interni della residenza. All'esterno, un porticato conduce ai giardini, sapientemente curati e conservati.

Location: **Florence, Italy**
Interior design: **Donatella Alessandri**
Photographer: © **Yael Pincus**

Feature space: Porch

164

The porch connects the house to the gardens. This charming, simple and elegant space is ideal for relaxing, chatting or simply contemplating the views.

Loggi stellt die Verbindung zwischen dem Haus und den Gärten her. Er hat einen ganz eigenen Charme und sein Dekor ist von Schlichter Eleganz. Hier kann man ausruhen, plaudern oder einfach nur die Aussicht genießen.

Le porche est un trait d'union entre la maison et les jardins. Cet espace au charme indéniable est décoré avec simplicité et élégance. C'est un havre de paix, où l'on se retire pour bavarder ou pour tout simplement jouir des vues.

El porche actúa como nexo entre la casa y los jardines. Este espacio posee gran encanto y está decorado con sencillez y elegancia. En él se puede descansar, charlar o simplemente disfrutar de las vistas.

Il porticato funge da nesso tra la casa e i giardini. Questo spazio, arredato in maniera semplice ma al contempo elegante possiede un fascino tutto particolare. Vi si può riposare, leggere, o semplicemente godere delle magnifiche viste.

The mural paintings are present in almost all corners of the home, giving them a great deal of color and volume. Unfortunately, some of these could not be restored. However the ones that remain visible enrich the villa and are evidence of its varied history throughout the centuries.

In fast alle Teilen des Hauses finden sich Wandmalereien, die Farbe in die Räume bringen und sie optisch erweitern. Leider konnten sie nicht überall erhalten werden, aber die noch sichtbaren bereichern die Villa als Zeugnisse eines jahrhundertelangen bewegten Lebens.

Les peintures murales, présentes dans presque tous les coins de l'habitation, apportent de la couleur et créent des effets de volume. Malheureusement, il n'a pas été possible de les conserver toutes, mais celles qui restent enrichissent la villa et sont un exemple évident de leur longue et merveilleuse vie au fil des siècles.

Las pinturas murales están presentes en casi todos los rincones de la vivienda, aportan color y crean efectos de volumen. Desgraciadamente, no han podido conservarse todas, pero las que se mantienen enriquecen la villa y son un ejemplo evidente de su magnífica y larga vida a lo largo de los siglos.

I dipinti murali, presenti in quasi tutti gli angoli dell'abitazione, apportano colore e creano effetti di volume. Sfortunatamente, non è stato possibile conservarli tutti, ma quelli rimasti arricchiscono lo stile della villa e sono un esempio evidente della loro lunga vita a dispetto dei secoli ormai trascorsi.

The gardens are another characteristic feature of the villa. Remarkably kept, they lend the residence a great deal of personality and provide the family with a private outdoor space which can only be admired from the porch and one of the wings of the house.

Die vornehmen gepflegten Gärten sind ein anderes Merkmal des Anwesens. Sie unterstreichen die Individualität des Hauses und bieten einen privaten Raum unter freiem Himmel für die Familie, der nur von der Loggia und einem Flügel des Hauses eingesehen werden kann.

Les jardins sont un des aspects qui définissent la villa. Elégants et soignés, ils donnent du caractère à la demeure et créent un espace ouvert, privé, pour la famille qui peut les admirer depuis l'atrium et une des ailes de la maison.

Los jardines son otra de las señas de identidad de la villa. Elegantes y cuidados, éstos aportan personalidad a la vivienda y proporcionan un espacio abierto y de uso privado para la familia que se puede admirar desde el porche y desde una de las alas de la casa.

I giardini sono un altro importante segno di identità della villa. Eleganti e ben curati, arricchiscono la personalità dell'abitazione e forniscono un gradevole spazio all'aperto e di uso privato per la famiglia, che li può ammirare dal porticato o da una delle ali della casa.

Eccentricity on the Mountainside

☐ This extravagant apartment offers a fantastic view of the winter holiday resort of Crans Montana, in Switzerland. The baroque interior is the result of the collaboration between the architect's imagination and the consent of the owners, a young Italian couple. The walls are bathed in a warm and sophisticated red Venetian stucco, while furniture pieces such as the leather headboard in the bedroom were especially designed for this residence. Other elements, like the horns used for hanging the lamps and appliqués, pay tribute to the geographical location of the villa. The captivating and unique interior is full of surprises and unexpected contrasts.

☐ Von diesem extravaganten Appartement aus hat man einen fantastischen Ausblick auf den Wintersportort Crans Montana in der Schweiz. Die originelle barocke Inneneinrichtung entstammt der Fantasie des Architekten und konnte mit dem Einverständnis der Besitzer, verwirklicht werden, einem jungen Paar aus Italien. Hervorzuheben sind der venezianische Stuck in einem ausgesucht warmen Rot und das für die Wohnung entworfene Mobiliar, z.B. das lederne Kopfende des Betts im Schlafzimmer. Geweihe als Lampenhalter verraten die geografische Lage des Chalets. Die Einrichtung ist originell und einfallsreich, voller Kontraste und Überraschungen.

☐ Cet appartement extravagant bénéficie de vues fantastiques sur le complexe de vacances d'hiver de Crans Montana, en Suisse. L'intérieur baroque et original est le fruit de l'imagination de l'architecte et de la complicité des propriétaires, un jeune couple italien. Le stuc vénitien, ressort dans une tonalité de rouge chaud et sophistiqué, ainsi que le mobilier conçu pour la résidence, à savoir, l'appui-tête en peau de la chambre de maîtres. D'autres éléments, comme les cornes pour accrocher les lampes et celles des appliques du mur, révèlent la situation géographique du chalet. L'intérieur est original et fascinant, rempli de surprises et de contrastes judicieux.

☐ Este extravagante apartamento disfruta de unas fantásticas vistas del complejo vacacional de invierno de Crans Montana, en Suiza. El interior barroco y original es fruto de la imaginación del arquitecto y de la complicidad de los propietarios, una joven pareja italiana. Destaca el estuco veneciano de un cálido y sofisticado color rojo, así como el mobiliario diseñado para esta residencia; por ejemplo, el cabezal de piel en el dormitorio principal. Otros elementos, como los cuernos para colgar lámparas y los de los apliques de la pared, delatan la situación geográfica del chalé. El interior es original y cautivador, lleno de sorpresas e ingeniosos contrastes.

☐ Questo stravagante appartamento gode di una vista magnifica sulla stazione turistica mondialmente rinomata di Crans Montana, in Svizzera. Gli interni in stile barocco e molto originali sono frutto dell'immaginazione dell'architetto e della complicità dei proprietari, una giovane coppia italiana. Da notare lo stucco veneziano in tonalità rossa calda e sofisticata, così come alcuni mobili, per esempio, la testata in pelle nella camera da letto principale. Altri elementi quali le corna per appendervi le lampade e le applique della parete ci indicano chiaramente la localizzazione geografica dello chalet. Gli interni sono affascinanti e singolari, pieni di sorprese e ingegnosi contrasti.

Location: **Crans Montana, Switzerland**
Architect: **Carlo Rampazzi**
Photographer: **© Reto Guntli / Zapaimages**

Feature space: **Dining room**

The small balcony offers a stunning view of the Alps, and during the warmer season, a small table transforms it into an outdoor terrace perfect for celebrating romantic dinners or meals with close friends.

Von einem kleinen Balkon aus hat man einen eindrucksvollen Blick auf die Alpen. Bei gutem Wetter wird hier mit einem kleinen Tisch ein Essplatz unter freiem Himmel geschaffen für romantische Abendessen oder anregende Mahlzeiten im kleinen Kreis.

Le petit balcon offre des vues impressionnantes sur les Alpes. Lorsque le temps le permet, une petite table peut convertir cet espace en une salle à manger extérieure pour célébrer des repas romantiques ou inviter un petit groupe réduit de personnes.

Desde el pequeño balcón pueden contemplarse impresionantes vistas de los Alpes. Cuando el tiempo es favorable, una pequeña mesa permite convertirlo en un comedor exterior y celebrar cenas románticas o comidas para un grupo reducido de personas.

Dal piccolo balcone è possibile godere delle sorprendenti viste delle Alpi. Quando le condizioni meteorologiche sono buone, un tavolino ci consente di allestire un piccolo angolo dove celebrare cene romantiche o pranzi per un gruppo ridotto di persone.

This theatrical dining room is distinguished by its furniture pieces such as the spectacular Lebanese cedar wood table surrounded by original seventies Knoll chairs upholstered in Fabergé fabrics. The space a futuristic style buffet and a retro lamp made of baccarat crystal.

Dieses theatralische Esszimmer besticht durch sein Mobiliar: einen spektakulären Tisch aus Zedernholz, um den originale Knollstühle aus den 70er-Jahren stehen, bezogen mit Stoffen von Fabergé. Ergänzt wird die Ausstattung durch eine futuristische Anrichte und Baccara-Lampen im Retrolook.

Cette salle à manger théâtrale, frappe par son mobilier : une table spectaculaire en cèdre du Liban est entourée de chaises Knoll originales, des années soixante, recouvertes de tissus de Fabergé. La pièce est compétée par un buffet futuriste et des lampes de cristal de baccarat, de style rétro.

Este teatral comedor destaca por su mobiliario: una espectacular mesa de cedro del Líbano está rodeada por sillas Knoll originales de los setenta, tapizadas con telas de Fabergé. La estancia se completa con un aparador de estilo futurista y unas lámparas de cristal de baccarat, de estética retro.

Questa teatrale sala da pranzo spicca per il suoi mobili: una spettacolare tavola in cedro del Libano con attorno sedie Knoll originali degli anni settanta, tappezzate con stoffe di Fabergé. La stanza si completa con una credenza in stile futurista e delle lampade di cristallo Baccarat, di estetica retrò.

Contemporary Luxury

☐ The Stern residence is a magnificent villa of nearly 16,000 square feet. In addition to the main residence, the property also includes a guest house, a pool and various stables. Its location gives the house a spectacular view of the North Salem valley, one of the area's greatest attractions. As an ideal mountain refuge, the design combines typical countryside elements with more modern ones in line with the owners' taste, such as their contemporary art collection. Materials like stone and cedar wood bring distinction and elegance to this modern and cozy home.

☐ Das prächtige Haus Stern ist fast 1500 m² groß. Neben dem eigentlichen Wohnhaus wurden noch weitere Gebäude errichtet: ein Gästehaus, Nebengebäude und ein Schwimmbad. Die Anlage des Hauses erlaubt es, den atemberaubenden Blick auf das Tal von North Salem zu genießen, der den Reiz dieses idyllischen Standorts ausmacht. Dieses Anwesen in den Bergen vereint Charakteristika eines Landhauses mit modernen Elementen, etwa den Werken zeitgenössischer Kunst, die seine Besitzer sammeln. Die verwendeten Materialien, Stein und Zedernholz, vermitteln eine vornehme Atmosphäre, sorgen für einen modernen Gesamteindruck und schaffen behagliche Räume.

☐ La résidence Stern est une ferme magnifique qui couvre environ 1.500 m². En plus de la maison, plusieurs édifices ont été construits : résidence d'amis, piscine et divers quartiers La disposition de la maison permet de bénéficier de vues spectaculaires sur la vallée de North Salem, un des points d'attraction du lieu. Ce site montagneux idyllique réunit les éléments propres à une maison de campagne et d'autres plus contemporains, en harmonie avec la personnalité des maîtres, à l'instar des œuvres de leur collection d'art contemporain. Les matériaux employés, pierre et bois de cèdre, affichent distinction, élégance et modernisme tout en créant des ambiances chaleureuses et accueillantes.

☐ La residencia Stern es una magnífica finca que tiene cerca de 1.500 m². Además de la casa, se han construido varios edificios: residencia de invitados, piscina y varias cuadras. La disposición de la casa permite disfrutar de espectaculares vistas al valle de North Salem, uno de los atractivos del lugar. Este idílico paraje de montaña reúne elementos propios de una casa de campo y otros más actuales y en consonancia con la personalidad de los dueños, como piezas de su colección de arte contemporáneo. Los materiales empleados, piedra y madera de cedro, otorgan distinción, elegancia y un aspecto moderno, y crean ambientes cálidos y acogedores.

☐ La residenza Stern è una magnifica tenuta grande circa 1.500 m². Oltre alla casa, sono stati costruiti vari edifici: la dependance per gli ospiti, la piscina e varie stalle. La disposizione della casa consente di godere di viste spettacolari sulla vallata del North Salem, una delle attrazioni del posto. Questo idillico posto di montagna abbina elementi tipici dell'architettura rurale con altri più moderni e consoni alla personalità dei proprietari, quali oggetti della loro collezione di arte contemporanea. I materiali adoperati, pietra e legno di cedro, conferiscono distinzione ed eleganza, un aspetto moderno e creano ambienti caldi ed accoglienti.

Location: **North Salem, New York, USA**
Architect: **Moro Stumper Associates**
Photographer: © **Scott Frances**

Feature space: **Patio**

In the evening, the patios exhibits its special charm. Its comfortable sofas and hammocks create an idea setting for relaxation, dreaming and enjoying the view. A fireplace allows cozy gatherings, even on cooler nights.

Am Abend verwandelt sich der Patio in einen Platz mit besonderem Charme. Bequeme Sofas und Liegestühle laden ein, die Aussicht zu genießen, zu entspannen und zu träumen. Durch den Kamin ist es möglich, diesen Ort auch an kalten Abenden für Plaudereien zu nutzen.

Les atriums se transforment, au crépuscule, en un lieu spécial. En plus des vues spectaculaires, les divans et hamacs confortables créent une atmosphère parfaite pour se relaxer et s'évader. Une cheminée permet de se réunir à l'extérieur, même lorsque les nuits sont froides.

Los porches se convierten, al atardecer, en un lugar especial. Además de las espectaculares vistas, los cómodos sofás y las hamacas crean una atmósfera perfecta para relajarse y evadirse. Una chimenea hace posible las tertulias en el exterior, incluso en las noches frías.

Al tramonto, i porticati diventano un posto davvero speciale. Oltre alle spettacolari vedute, i comodi divani e le amache creano un'atmosfera perfetta per rilassarsi ed evadere un attimo dalla realtà. Un caminetto favorisce incontri e ritrovi all'aperto persino nelle serate più fredde.

The bathrooms are decorated the countryside style, with the additions of numerous modern elements. In one of the bathrooms, for example, a unique metal basin lends an antique feel. The presence of earth shades and wood contribute to the warmth of the space.

Obwohl die Badezimmer der Ästhetik des Landhausstils verpflichtet sind, wird nicht auf moderne Elemente verzichtet. In einem der Bäder sorgt ein metallenes Handwaschbecken für eine gewisse Nostalgie. Warme Farbtöne und Holz tragen das ihre zur Schaffung eines behaglichen Gesamteindrucks bei.

Les salles de bains conservent l'esthétique propre aux maisons de campagne, tout en bénéficiant d'équipements modernes : une des salles de bains, par exemple, conserve un certain aspect ancien grâce à un lave-mains original en métal. Los tons ocres et le bois contribuent à créer un univers chaleureux.

Los baños conservan la estética propia de las casas de campo, pero añadiendo unas modernas prestaciones; uno de los baños, por ejemplo, consigue cierto aspecto antiguo mediante un original lavamanos de metal. Los tonos tierra y la madera contribuyen a crear un ambiente cálido.

I bagni mantengono l'estetica propria delle case di campagna, con l'aggiunta però di qualche elemento e prestazione moderna. In uno dei bagni, per esempio, è presente un lavamano originale che dà un leggero aspetto antico. I toni color terra e il legno danno calore a tutto l'ambiente.

A Noble Residence

☐ This majestic residence is an example of luxury and grandness. The rooms are decorated in great detail and adorned with exquisite furnishings, objects and fabrics. A small bench next to a window, cushions and curtains in warm tones, and a hallway decorated with oriental objects are just a few examples of what can be found inside this home. The rustic kitchen features copper kitchenware and a collection of porcelain vases. Delicate furniture pieces decorate the hallways and living areas, enhancing the noble aspect of this house.

☐ Dieses majestätische Anwesen ist ein Beispiel für Luxus und Grandiosität. Alle Räume sind bis ins kleinste Detail durchdacht und mit ausgesuchten Möbeln, Dekorationsobjekten und Stoffen ausgestattet. Eine kleine Bank unter einem Fenster mit Kissen und Vorhängen in warmen Tönen und ein mit orientalischen Gegenständen dekorierter Flur sind nur ein kleiner Vorgeschmack auf das, was einen im Rest des Hauses erwartet. In der Küche im Landhausstil hängt das kupferne Kochgeschirr über der Mittelinsel, und auf einem Regal steht eine Sammlung von Porzellankrügen. Feine Möbel schmücken Flure und Salons und unterstreichen den herrschaftlichen Charakter des Hauses.

☐ Cette majestueuse résidence est un exemple de luxe et de grandeur. Toutes les pièces sont soignées dans les moindres détails et décorées de meubles exquis, d'objets et de tapisseries. Un petit banc à côté d'une fenêtre, paré de coussins et de rideaux aux tons chaleureux, et un petit couloir décoré d'objets orientaux ne sont qu'un exemple dans la maison parmi tant d'autres. La cuisine, de style champêtre, dispose d'une batterie de cuisine en cuivre au-dessus de l'îlot de travail et une collection de jarres de porcelaine sur la console. Des meubles délicats décorent les couloirs et salons exaltant l'air seigneurial de la maison.

☐ Esta majestuosa residencia es un ejemplo de lujo y grandiosidad. Todas las estancias cuidan hasta el más mínimo detalle y están decoradas con exquisitos muebles, objetos y tapicerías. Un pequeño banco junto a una ventana, con cojines y cortinas de tonos cálidos, y un pasillo decorado con objetos orientales son sólo una pequeña muestra de lo que se encuentra en el resto de la casa. La cocina, de estilo campestre, tiene menaje de cobre sobre la isla de trabajo y una colección de jarrones de porcelana en la repisa. Delicadas piezas de mobiliario decoran los pasillos y salones y acentúan el aire señorial de la casa.

☐ Questa maestosa residenza è un esempio di lusso e grandiosità. Tutti gli ambienti sono stati curati nei minimi particolari e arredati con mobili raffinati, tappezzerie e oggetti di qualità. Una piccola panca posta accanto alla finestra, con cuscini e tende dai toni caldi, e un corridoio arredato con oggetti orientali sono soltanto un esempio di ciò che possiamo trovare nel resto della casa. La cucina, in stile rustico, è adornata con utensili in rame disposti lungo il piano di lavoro e una collezione di vasi di porcellana che occupa la mensola. L'arredamento è affidato a mobili delicati e raffinati che decorano i corridoi e i saloni accentuando l'atmosfera signorile della residenza.

Location: **Oxfordshire, UK**
Interior design: **Alison Henry**
Photographer: © **Andreas von Einsiedel**

Feature space: **Main bedroom**

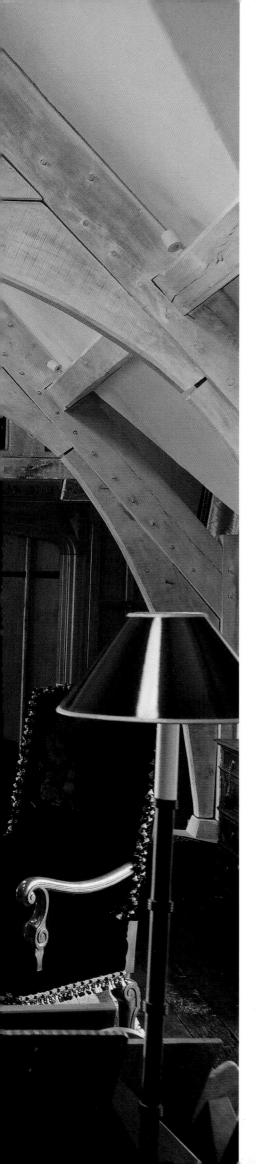

The master bedroom is a majestic room that boasts a canopy bed with extravagantly dark drapery that matches the sofa, armchairs and window curtains. Antique bureaux and trunks decorate the space and create a distinguished atmosphere.

Das Schlafzimmer ist ein prächtiger Raum mit einem Himmelbett mit schweren dunklen Vorhängen; dazu passen das Sofa, die Sessel und die Vorhänge an den Fenstern. Kommoden und antike Truhen verleihen dem Zimmer eine distinguierte Atmosphäre.

La chambre de maîtres est une majestueuse pièce où l'on remarque un lit à baldaquin et de somptueux rideaux foncés, assortis au divan, aux fauteuils et au rideau de la baie vitrée. Commodes et malles anciennes décorent la pièce, créant une atmosphère distinguée.

El dormitorio principal es una majestuosa estancia donde destacan una cama con dosel y suntuosos cortinajes oscuros, a juego con el sofá, las butacas y la cortina que cubre el ventanal. Cómodas y baúles antiguos decoran la estancia y crean una atmósfera distinguida.

La camera da letto principale è una stanza ampia dove spicca un letto a baldacchino e sontuosi tendaggi scuri che fanno pendant con il divano, le poltrone e la tenda che copre il finestrone. Ad arricchire ulteriormente l'ambiente ci pensano delle cassettiere e bauli d'antiquariato.

The child's bedroom is a beautiful room especially designed for the younger ones; doll houses and lively bedspreads make it the perfect play room, while maintaining the air of distinction and elegance that reigns throughout the household.

Das hübsche Kinderschlafzimmer ist eigens für die Kleinsten eingerichtet. Puppenhäuser und lustig bedruckte Stoffe auf den Betten laden hier zum Spielen ein, ohne dass auf die vornehme Eleganz verzichtet würde, die in dem gesamten Anwesen herrscht.

La chambre à coucher des enfants est une pièce adorable conçue tout spécialement pour les tout petits: maisons de poupées et imprimés amusants sur les lits font de ce lieu un espace idéal pour jouer, sans renoncer à l'élégance et la distinction qui dominent dans toute la résidence.

El dormitorio infantil es una preciosa habitación pensada especialmente para los más pequeños; casas de muñecas y divertidos estampados sobre las camas hacen de este lugar un espacio perfecto para jugar, sin renunciar a la elegancia y la distinción que impera en toda la residencia.

Alcuni oggetti della camera da letto dei bambini rivelano a prima vista i suoi occupanti: case di bambole, giocattoli e copriletti dagli stampati divertenti. Una stanza amena e ideale per giocare, che non rinuncia però all'eleganza e signorilità che regna in tutta la dimora.

Like a Palace

☐ This luxurious residence in Sussex boasts a grand exterior and a neoclassical architecture. A luminous interior and classic decoration characterizes this residence, which displays elegant and distinguished furniture pieces. A magnificent entrance hall leads to the living areas and a staircase lined with a red carpet. The armchairs create warm and homely spaces, as do the curtains, whose great detail and quality do not go unnoticed. The small living room, furnished with outdoor furniture, is surrounded by plants and delicate curtains that diffuse the light entering through the windows.

☐ Mit seiner klassizistischen Architektur stellt sich das Äußere dieses prachtvollen Anwesens in Sussex hochherrschaftlich dar. Die hellen, klassisch eingerichteten Innenräumen sind vornehm mit distinguiertem Mobiliar ausgestattet. Von einem eindrucksvollen Vestibül aus erreicht man die einzelnen Räume und eine Treppe mit rotem Teppich. In den einladenden Räumen mit ihren Sesseln und Sofas zeigt sich der Luxus in den wertvollen Stoffen der Vorhänge. Der kleine Salon mit den Gartenmöbeln ist von Pflanzen umgeben, und die zarten Gardinen dämpfen das Licht, das durch die großen Fenster hereinfällt.

☐ Cette résidence luxueuse du Sussex exhibe un extérieur seigneurial et une architecture néoclassique. Dotée d'un intérieur très lumineux et d'une décoration classique, la maison affiche un mobilier élégant et très distingué. Un magnifique vestibule distribue les pièces et mène à un escalier doté d'un tapis rouge. Les sièges et fauteuils créent des salles chaudes et accueillantes, où le luxe se manifeste dans les détails des rideaux et tissus de qualité supérieure. Le petit salon, doté de meubles d'extérieur, est entouré de plantes, et des rideaux tout en délicatesse tamisent la lumière qui entre par les baies vitrées.

☐ Esta lujosa residencia en Sussex exhibe un exterior señorial y una arquitectura neoclásica. Con un interior muy luminoso y una decoración clásica, la casa muestra un mobiliario elegante y muy distinguido. Un magnífico vestíbulo articula las estancias y conduce a una escalera con una alfombra roja. Los sillones y butacas crean salas cálidas y acogedoras, en las que el lujo se descubre en los detalles de las cortinas y telas de gran calidad. El pequeño salón, con muebles de exterior, está rodeado de plantas, y unas delicadas cortinas tamizan la luz que entra a través de los ventanales.

☐ Questa lussuosa residenza nel Sussex sfoggia degli esterni signorili e un'architettura neoclassica. La mobilia elegante e molto singolare tende verso un arredamento di stampo classico. Un magnifico vestibolo articola le varie stanze e conduce a una scala con tappeto rosso. I divani e le poltrone creano sale dai toni caldi e accoglienti, dove il lusso si fa evidente nei particolari delle tende e delle pregiate stoffe. Il piccolo salone, arredato con mobili per esterni, è circondato da piante e delle sottili tende filtrano la luce che passa attraverso le grandi finestre.

Location: **Sussex, UK**
Interior design: **John Simpson**
Photographer: © **Andreas von Einsiedel**

Feature space: **Entrance hall**

The entrance hall is an example of the luxury of this residence. The dome that presides this area lends light to the space and creates and an exquisitely noble impression. Various vases are placed on the shelves above the arches that crown the four sides of this foyer.

Das Vestibül vermittelt einen Eindruck vom Luxus dieses Anwesens. Eine Kuppel erfüllt den Raum mit Licht und sorgt für einen bewundernswert vornehmen Eindruck. Jede der vier Seiten des Raumes ist mit einem Bogen geschmückt, über dem jeweils eine Vase auf einer Konsole steht.

Le vestibule est un exemple du luxe qui se dégage de cette résidence. La coupole qui préside cette pièce confère luminosité à l'espace et crée une touche seigneuriale délicieuse. De nombreux vases sont placés sur les consoles installées sur les arcs couronnant les quatre côtés de cette antichambre.

El vestíbulo es un ejemplo del lujo que se respira en esta residencia. La cúpula que preside esta estancia aporta luminosidad al espacio y crea un exquisito ambiente señorial. Varios jarrones asoman en las repisas situadas sobre los arcos que coronan los cuatro lados de este recibidor.

L'atrio è un esempio del lusso che si respira in questa dimora. La cupola che presiede questa stanza apporta luminosità allo spazio e dà un tocco squisitamente signorile. Diversi vasi spuntano dalle mensole collocate sugli archi che coronano i quattro lati di questo ingresso.

The bedroom is simple and elegant, achieving a balance between luxury and simplicity. The furniture is classical in style and decorative objects are scarce; the white closet and the bed stand out the most.

Das schlichte Schlafzimmer stellt ein gelungenes Gleichgewicht zwischen Einfachheit und Luxus dar. Die Möbel sind klassisch, und es gibt kaum Schmuckobjekte. Der weiße Schrank und das Bett sind die bedeutendsten Möbelstücke.

La chambre à coucher est une pièce sobre et élégante qui réussit à trouver l'équilibre parfait entre luxe et sobriété. Les meubles sont de style classique et les objets de décoration sont à peine existants : l'armoire blanche et le lit sont les deux éléments qui ressortent le plus.

El dormitorio es una estancia sencilla y elegante que consigue un equilibrio entre lujo y simplicidad. Los muebles son de estilo clásico y apenas hay objetos decorativos; el armario de color blanco y la cama son los dos elementos que más destacan.

L'arredamento della camera da letto denota un voluto equilibrio tra semplicità ed eleganza. Gli oggetti decorativi sono ridotti al minimo indispensabile; tra i mobili, in stile classico, spiccano l'armadio di colore bianco e il letto.

Rural Style in the Open Country

☐ This English residence is distinguished by classic-style sumptuous interiors. The house features of two living areas with fireplaces, a large kitchen that is connected to the dining area and a luxurious master bedroom with en suite bathroom. The large windows give a unique character to the facade and allow natural light to penetrate the interiors. Furnished with antique pieces, oil paintings and fresh, colorful flowers, the rooms breathe an exquisite elegance. The living room gives onto the garden, where the tenants can enjoy the marvelous landscape and natural surroundings.

☐ Dieses englische Landhaus birgt prachtvolle, im klassischen Stil eingerichtete Räume. Es verfügt über zwei Wohnzimmer mit Kamin, eine geräumige Küche, die mit dem Esszimmer verbunden ist, und ein prächtiges Schlafzimmer mit Bad en Suite. Die großen Fenster sind charakteristisch für die Fassade und lassen viel Tageslicht in die Innenräume. Die Zimmer erhalten ihre ausgesuchte Eleganz durch antike Stücke, Ölgemälde und frische Blumen, die Farbe und Vitalität vermitteln. Vom Salon aus gelangt man in den Garten, wo man die Natur und die herrliche Landschaft genießen kann.

☐ Cette résidence anglaise affiche de somptueuses pièces décorées dans le style classique. La maison est composée de deux salons, chacun possédant une cheminée, une vaste cuisine qui communique avec la zone de la salle à manger et une luxueuse chambre de maîtres avec une salle de bains, à l'instar d'une suite. Les grandes fenêtres donnent du caractère à la façade et permettent à la lumière naturelle d'inonder les pièces. Meublés à l'ancienne avec des portraits à l'huile et des fleurs fraîches apportant couleur et vitalité, les espaces sont d'une élégance exquise. Du salon, on accède au jardin extérieur, d'où l'on peut profiter du paysage magnifique et de la nature.

☐ Esta residencia inglesa muestra unas suntuosas estancias decoradas con un estilo clásico. La casa se compone de dos salones, ambos con chimenea, una amplia cocina que comunica con la zona del comedor y un lujoso dormitorio principal con el baño en suite. Las grandes ventanas aportan singularidad a la fachada y permiten que la luz natural inunde las estancias. Amueblados con piezas decorativas antiguas, retratos al óleo y flores frescas que dan color y vitalidad, los espacios son de una elegancia exquisita. Desde el salón se accede al jardín exterior, donde se puede disfrutar del magnífico paisaje y de la naturaleza.

☐ Questa residenza inglese mostra stanze sontuose arredate in uno stile classico. La casa è formata da due saloni, entrambi con caminetto, un'ampia cucina che comunica con la sala da pranzo e una lussuosa camera da letto principale con bagno suite. Le grandi finestre apportano singolarità alla facciata e consentono alla luce naturale di inondare abbondantemente le stanze. Gli spazi, arredati con pezzi d'epoca, ritratti ad olio e fiori freschi che danno colore e vitalità, sono di un'eleganza squisita. Dal salone si accede al giardino esterno, dove si può godere del magnifico paesaggio e della natura circostante.

Location: Hampshire, UK
Interior design: Kate Pols
Photographer: © Andreas von Einsiedel

Feature space: Bedroom

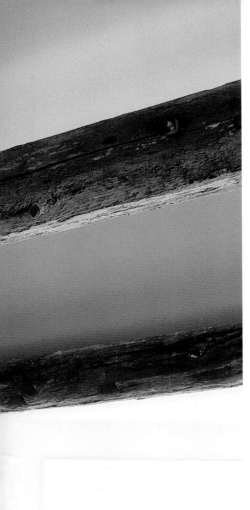

The master bedroom on the first floor is a spacious area furnished with an elegant chaise longue next to the windows, a fireplace and an impressive canopy bed. The bathroom, situated under a sloping ceiling, features original fixtures and objects

Das Schlafzimmer liegt im ersten Stock. Es ist ein großzügiger Raum mit einer eleganten Chaiselongue am Fenster, einem Kamin und einem Himmelbett. Das Bad liegt unter der Dachschräge und besitzt noch eine originale Einrichtung.

La chambre de maîtres, au premier étage, est une large pièce, dotée d'une élégante chaise longue près des baies vitrées, d'une cheminée et d'un imposant lit à baldaquin. La salle de bains, dans la partie mansardée, est dotée d'œuvres originales.

El dormitorio principal, en el primer piso, es una estancia amplia, con un elegante chaise longe junto a los ventanales, una chimenea y una imponente cama con dosel. El baño, en la zona abuhardillada, contiene piezas originales.

Al primo piano, la camera da letto principale è molto ampia, con un'elegante chaise longue posta accanto alle finestre, un caminetto e un imponente letto a baldacchino. Il bagno, situato nella zona mansardata, contiene alcuni pezzi originali.

The fireplaces lend a grand atmosphere to the residence, giving it also an homely feeling, especially during winter time. The warmth of a fireplace can be felt not only in the living rooms, but also in the master bedroom and even in the small dining room.

Die Kamine lassen die Wohnung herrschaftlicher erscheinen und machen sie behaglicher, vor allem im Winter. In diesem Haus kann man sich das ganze Jahr über nicht nur in den Wohnzimmern des Kaminfeuers erfreuen, sondern auch im Schlafzimmer und sogar im kleinen Esszimmer.

Les cheminées confèrent à la demeure un aspect seigneurial, la rendant plus accueillante, spécialement en hiver. Dans cette résidence, il est possible de bénéficier de la chaleur du foyer au fil des saisons, à l'instar de la chambre de maîtres, du salon et même d'une petite salle à manger.

Las chimeneas otorgan un aspecto señorial a una vivienda y la hacen más acogedora, especialmente en invierno. En esta residencia, es posible disfrutar del calor del hogar en varias estancias, como el dormitorio principal, el salón o incluso un pequeño comedor.

I caminetti danno un aspetto signorile all'abitazione rendendola ancora più accogliente specialmente nei mesi invernali. In questa dimora, l'atmosfera familiare si respira in varie stanze, quali la camera da letto principale, il salone o persino una piccola sala da pranzo.